UHMANDRA

(UH – MUN – DRUH)

A Story

By

C. Schmidt

UHMANDRA

Special shout out to the genuine people I have met over the past few years; the few who have been transparent with me and haven't used their personal agendas to dictate the course of our relationship.

Teamwork at its finest.

Peace.

- C.

UHMANDRA

PROLOGUE

Disorder and confusion has taken over Hock City after Langston - the strange, human visitor - arrived. Humans have been gone for some time; the others who remain have been hidden. Only a few know he is human, however, while The Guardian of Hock City wants to keep it that way. This surprising and shocking visit caused an unexpected headache, triggering The Guardian to abruptly evacuate and lock down the city in order to find the human intruder. His impatience with the chase has grown, creating a frenzy for those around him.

Because of these events, the activity inside the walls is no longer normal, as if one could actually use the word normal to describe what happens here.

Langston's only goals are to survive and find his way back home. Although, he needs more time and help in order to reach these goals.

His mission has affected several others, fueling and reigniting some desires of the new people he has met. He had no idea that his journey would incorporate other lives, especially in this magnitude.

Langston gets closer to discovering the true whereabouts of his home, Uhmandra, with assistance from Jesse, Kinth, Miles and some others. More importantly, he discovers who he is.

"Your journey is the journey of many."

Tension Soaks the Air

WAIT TILL HE SEES THIS, he thinks. The goods dealer can't break free from his lustful, obsessive gaze. Smiling at the gun he is holding, he inhales an odor from a fresh firing and the residue of gun smoke. The glare from the sun bounces off of the fine weaponry.

The sun sits high at the moment as rays beam above Pineville and Hock City. Brighter than usual, deceiving some into thinking it plans to stay a while.

Shamefully, the goods dealer looks around Pineville's busy streets which are full of locals going about their day. He watches them closely, ensuring that no one sees the emotion he wears on his face.

It reflects an expression somewhat similar to the funny clown mask he found during one of his runs in the past. He had to really dig to find this mask, because it had fallen behind some shelving and was hidden behind cobwebs. He struggles to conceal his excitement about the item.

Swiftly he makes his way back toward the heart of the Pines which is near Hock City's main gate, the outskirts. It was once a free-for-all area where it was first-come-first serve, meant for those who wanted to survive. Necessities were scarce, unless you had the lines or the wit. Or the muscle to take what you wanted. Better yet, the abilities. Sometimes, it was just who you knew.

To a degree, this part of the Pines was a replica of Hock City - just smaller in size and nowhere near as pretty. And, it was populated with less people. Poor people. An expendable society where if you were fortunate to be on the outside looking in, as some say. Or rather, on the inside of the walls.

The goods dealer had to beat the darkness he expected to arrive, thereby preparing for the cold temperatures that would accompany it. The sun was unpredictable. At times it hid behind a modified troposphere. He wasn't too fooled by its presence. And the dark brought trouble, seemingly, most of the time.

While some nights it was quiet, he didn't want to take that chance again. The last time he did he had paid the price. He survived, but by the skin of his teeth. The deep slash wounds on his chest reminded him of that price daily. He got a little too close to Snake Valley.

He pushes his cart - full of now meaningless items which he didn't care if he would see again, except for one. The most important piece of hardware he had come across in a while. A reward from a deal of which he couldn't imagine happening again. He couldn't stop staring at it with irreverent eyes. The weapon; the gun from the large wanderer who he met while north of Hock.

Should I sell it or keep it? he thinks deeply. Keeping it meant he would not acquire any lines for it, lines which would get him more important rations like the food he and his family needed. He would not receive the required sustenance to survive in sometimes an incredibly harsh environment. And clothing; good clothing – not the scraps he normally found when he ventured into the wilderness.

He was once a member of Hock City's workforce, working for the water collection plant. This was how he was able to join the line system. But when he fell on harder times, he was forced outside the walls to live amongst the others.

He forcefully strokes his chin, thinking about the decision at hand. After a couple of deep, heavy breaths, he adjusts his thoughts and presses forward. One foot in front of the other, with his eyes watching his surroundings. He walks for some time before he finally makes it to his home.

"Hey, neighbor! Peace and light! " The sound of a husky voice breaks his concentration. "Find anything good since ya left?" The gregarious onlooker yells at him from the distance. The square-bodied, aging man – wearing glasses with thick lenses - fumbles through containers on his front steps. Kicking an empty plastic jug out of frustration, he hollers inside at someone who was speaking to him. "Shut up! I know! I know! I will ask 'em!"

"Peace and light!" responds the goods dealer. "Nope! None this time!" he adds, short of words. Normally he would be forthcoming and excited to barter his latest finds, but not this time. He battles with the idea of keeping the new loot for himself. Keeping this in mind, his pace grows faster. He didn't want to be cornered in a game of twenty-two questions. "Gotta get in. This sun is beginning to fade. Seems like the dark is coming. You should do the same! Not a good idea to be out here when ya can't see your feet in front of ya!"

His neighbor watches his movements closely. The yellowy glaze of his eyes are amplified through his glasses.

"Yeah, no lie there. Sky does look that way. But, all right! Lemme take a look at what you got at the Exchange. You comin,' right? Somebody stole my goddamn hammer! Me and my brother need one to do some fixin' 'round here. Those sand storms can be brutal on the house. Look at my goddamn roof! If you have one, lemme trade ya for it! Or loan it for something I got."

The goods dealer waves his hand at his neighbor in confirmation. Turning his head in front of him, he sees his wife just yards away. She is sweeping debris from their front porch. He waves at her, but then motions for her to go inside of their home as he approaches. Slightly perturbed, she looks at him. After being together for most of their adult lives, she can tell something is on his mind.

"What's wrong? Did you have trouble again? Did somebody do somethin' to you?" she asks with emphasis.

"Go, go. C'mon. Hurry in. Close the door." The goods dealer shoos his wife inside as he quickly pushes his cart through the narrow opening of the home. He hurries before anyone else outdoors could see him, hardly able to contain his excitement. He does a little dance as he makes his way indoors, watching his wife pull the rickety door closed behind him.

A full or blanket-covered cart often times meant all eyes were on you, especially if you weren't mingling with other people with the intent to exchange some of your goods. These types of carts were raided at any available moment, even if bartering was intended. The goods dealer's rules are simple: Keep your eyes on your shit, and don't expose too much.

"Oh - you must have hit the jackpot this time, Eli!" his wife exclaims, widening her smile to show some of her teeth. Her excitement exuded a radiant glow from her skin, resembling small specks of floating glitter.

"Shh. I did. Where is Junior? Call him in here."

"In his room," she replies before turning her attention away. "Junior! Honey! Come here, please."

"Why?!" Junior yells from the distance.

"NOW, Junior!" Mom snaps back.

"Shh. Not so loud," Eli adds.

"Okay, okay. *Goodness.* You are making me nervous."

"No need to be nervous, dear," Eli replies.

"You know, I had to get on him today."

"Why?" Eli moves his items around in the cart, mentally cataloging everything he acquired and figuring out each item's cost.

"He told on himself."

"What you mean, 'told on himself'?"

"I heard your son talking about stuff he shouldn't have to his little friends out there. Had to get on him. But, I will let *him* . . . tell you what happened," Eli's wife says, leaning against the kitchen counter softly.

"Oh boy," Eli scoffs.

"Wassup?" Junior excitedly enters the room, tossing a small ball back and forth in his hands.

"*What's up?*" Eli turns and sternly repeats his son's question. "Are we inside with the family, or outdoors with our friends?"

"Sorry. Hi, Dad."

"That's better. I found something for both of you. Took some doing, but I had a little luck this run." Eli reaches into his cart, where he pulls out a woman's cloche hat which he found on a shabby, battered mannequin. "For *Momma*," he said, with a smile, as he hands the hat to his wife. He then digs deeper into the pile of goods, shifting them around more. "For my son," He grabs a wooden plane toy, which has a dinged wing.

"Oh, wow! Thanks, Dad!" Junior tosses the plane into the air. The plane stays suspended above him. He moves it without touching it with his hands, while making a weird sound with his mouth. He mimics what he thinks a plane sounds like before darting off towards his room. Before he can get far, he is summoned once more.

"Wait a minute. Don't go anywhere yet," Eli insists.

Junior turns around to face him, his eyes wide with his mouth partially open.

"Eli, as much as I like this, shouldn't we trade it for something more important?" Mom removes the hat from her head, looking at it fondly.

"Don't you worry about that. I got something more important already."

As Eli finishes his statement, he grabs the handle to the shotgun and pulls the gun out slowly. His wife takes notice. Frowning, she takes a step back. Junior's eyebrows shoot to the top of his head. He can see some of his reflection in the gun.

"Should I sell it? Or keep it?"

"Wow, Dad! Where you get it?" With excitement in his eyes, Junior reaches out to touch the gun.

Mom quickly blocks Junior's hand, pulling him back beside her. "Be careful with that, Eli. How did you get that? What did you do? Did you do some-"

"It's not loaded, baby. I didn't do anything. It was practically given to me."

"Nobody in their right mind is going to just give you something like that. What did you trade? Did you make a promise you can't keep? Junior, cover your ears." Mom orders before leaning towards Eli. "Did you steal that? Please don't tell me that, Eli."

Junior pretends to cover his ears but is still listening.

"No, no, no, no," Eli replies, with a mildly frustrated tone.

"Are you sure?" Mom folds her arms as she takes a step closer toward the table.

"Yes! I traded an old cloth and some clothing. Can you believe that? I got this for a cloth! Just because the cloth had some weird markings on it," Eli spoke with a gut-full of jolly.

"No. I don't. I believe *you*, but I don't trust whoever that person was. Just odd. Sounds like a transaction out of desperation. Desperation that could bring something negative our way. We don't need any more issues 'round here."

Eli scoffs again, waving off his wife's comments.

"You goin' keep it, Dad?"

"Enough about that thing. Tell your dad what you did."

Junior lowers his chin and stares at his toy plane.

"*Junior.*"

"I stayed up pass my bedtime," Junior sighs.

"*And?*"

"I was looking out the window when it was dark outside."

"Junior, you know better. Right? I'm sure your mother already got on you about it. Don't do it again. We are just trying to keep you safe. Understand?"

"Yeah."

"*Yeah?*"

"Yes, sir."

"That's better. Go play," Eli pushes his son playfully. Junior giggles before jetting down the hall with the plane floating in front of him.

"You always let him off so easy, Eli."

Eli laughs quietly to himself. "He's just a boy; let him be. He's curious is all. No different than I was when I was his age. And you, too."

"Mmm hmm. Don't laugh at him. It's not funny. You are gone a lot, and I need him to listen to me when you aren't here. With all the madness out there, I don't need it in here, too."

"Okay, dear."

"I'm serious, Eli."

"I know. I know you are."

A tense quiet fills the room. Eli gives his wife a quick peck on the cheek before admiring the gun more. His wife serves him a small meal of stew on a plate made of wood which included leftover wild rabbit meat, potatoes and vegetables. A meal that they didn't have often. It was only available when Eli had enough quality items to trade for this type of spread. Or when he was lucky enough to actually land some game during a hunt.

"He saw something out there, Eli."

"Who? Saw what?" Eli is distracted by his goods again. He can barely eat.

"Junior. He saw something outside . . . near that road . . . What is it? 99? When he was up late."

"What'd he see?"

"Nothing good. He said something about a large man fighting those sand people. And some other man. I guess the large man was helping the smaller man. I don't know. Just a buncha mess."

Wrinkles crease across Eli's brow as he rubs the gun with a hand towel. The more his wife speaks about what Junior saw, the more he looks at the weapon; as if there was more to his transaction with the wanderer than that of which he was aware.

"I – " he shakes his head. "I'm sure whatever it was is over. Its fine, honey. Don't worry."

"I hope so. Put that thing away and eat before your food gets cold. Please."

Not too far away, alarms roar throughout Hock City's streets, sending most people in the area into a frantic. Tension soaks the air, causing extreme moments of confusion. The wailing of the sirens is an annoyance to those around, so much so that people pick fights with one another. Commands are issued over loud speakers, which are strategically positioned on several buildings, in various corners of the busy Line District.

"Attention please. Attention. Citizens of Hock City. Under the orders of The Guardian, all patrons of this city must exit through the main gates. Please move in an orderly fashion. Again - under the orders of The Guardian, all patrons of Hock City must exit through the main gates. Please move in an orderly fashion. Those who do not comply will face consequences. Attention please. . ."

People scramble for last minute bets inside of the casinos along 777 Place and North Diamond Drive, as the orders are repeated every few minutes. Others run to their temporary hostel rooms, hiding where they can to avoid having to leave. No one wants to deal with life outside of the walls.

Some fight back, using their various abilities to contest the guards. Most are unsuccessful.

"Examine every inch of this retched place! Do what you have to . . . to find the intruders!" The Mantis speaks to a group of guards sternly, watching the madness build around him.

"Roger that," the unit's captain replies.

The guards spread out to scour the various parts of the casino.

"Let's go, people! Shut it down! Shut it all down! Live to see another day! Enjoy more freedoms! Or meet your demise! Your choice!"

"Get moving! Don't make me say it again!" a lieutenant scowls.

Pushing and shoving; violent actions repeated even to those who are complying. Weapons are fired into the air to cause further panic.

"Close the vaults! Lock up the lines! No more issued! No more betting!"

The once loyal henchmen of Madam Pearl were now under a new direction from The Guardian: lock down the city. No one could come in and everyone - except for a few – must leave. The large group of uniformed men, women and creatures swarm the grounds, enjoying every moment available to strong-arm the people under their control.

Only those who are employed in critical, mission-related positions can remain inside the gate. Essential positions, such as gate guards, perimeter patrols and members of The Guardian's Special Forces were permitted. Other positions such as water collection and food preparation employees, along with handpicked individuals by The Guardian himself also remained. Those not on the list were pushed from the cleaner streets of the Line District to outside its entrance.

At this point, everyone has a choice: be reviewed, questioned and potentially quarantined. Be scanned for human elements or be banned. Banished from the gates and pushed away from things that enabled their addictions. Moreover, they were banished from their needs, desires and comfortable living.

The search was for anyone human, or for anyone that looked suspicious enough to be accused of being human. Daunting tasks with urgency behind them that grew quickly like weeds. Almost everyone was questioned.

If you were against being examined, you were thrown outside of the walls. Back into the not-so warm embrace of the Pines, to an environment where people fought over scraps and murdered each other over goods.

Back to an area that had even bigger threats, such as the creatures lurking mostly when it was dark. They captured people whom are never seen again thereafter. In a land that was more than just a little unsafe.

Or, you were just killed on the spot.

Starting first with Madam Pearl's place, the guards swiftly close each venue within the Line District with help from a new set of Mantodea and Blattos soldiers. Casino goers and guests are forced from the building without an explanation. Shouting and boisterous swearing ring inside of the dimly lit rooms, as people are man-handled and forced to the exits.

All of these actions are executed without the word 'human' being used once by the guards. Instead, there are 'thieves' and 'intruders' on the loose. The guards were searching for them, as well as for anyone with clues on their whereabouts.

Two thieves: a short one and a tall one. The taller one wasn't from the city and 'looked different.' This was the only vague information provided.

Where is the human?

A pair of guards spoke to one another quietly as they complete their required orders.

"Status. See anything suspicious?"

"Nah, man. All these people I've seen before. Nobody out of the norm."

"Yeah, they ain't here. I don't think they here."

"Why would they be? Why would they come back to where we could find them easy?"

"True," the second guard thinks deeply, examining his weapon. He turns it on and off, still fascinated with its sound after having used it a million times before.

"You're goin' to drain your battery," the other guard notices. He then revisits the earlier comments. "Or, maybe that's how they want us to think. To trick us."

"Doubt it. Nobody 'round here that smart."

"So where do you think they are?"

"If they are smart, headed far from this place."

"Yeah, that's what I would do. But to where, though?"

"Man, who knows? All I know is . . . nothing good coming from this."

"Not a damn thing."

Contingencies

THE LIGHT FROM THE CELLAR FADES. The mild glow from the room moves away from the group's concerned faces. They think intensely about what is next for them, as well as what is next for Kinth. The weary thoughts lay on their minds so thick that they could be cut with a knife.

"Will he be okay?" asks Jesse.

"That guy? *Please*. He will be fine," replies Miles.

"They got Madam Pearl, too."

"Stop worrying."

"I thought you said you made the tunnels large enough for me to fit, too?" asks Langston. He frustratingly shakes his head. "How am I supposed to get through this? I'm not trying to walk like this the whole way." Langston walks bent over, moving his head to avoid bumping it on the soil above him.

Miles, visibly aggravated by the comments, stops in his tracks. "You know, human, you awfully picky. Looking at the fact that you could still be back there; waiting on whatever that guy had planned for you. You should be praising me! Not questioning my actions. A little patience at the least."

"Can we just keep goin,' *please*?" Jesse interjects, pointing his finger in front of him. "This way, right? *Right?*"

"Yeah, kid. That way."

"I'm just saying," Langston continues.

The group presses on; forward into the mostly murky, dirt-lined tunnels. Different tunnels from what Jesse and Langston had once traveled. These tunnels are neither guarded by the gatekeepers nor have multiple floating doorways. All they have is . . . darkness, at least at the moment.

The ground around and above the tunnel is punctured with small holes, which let in a small amount of natural light and air. The cave-like environment has the ability to hold onto to the light that travels into its core from above ground. It provides just enough illumination for Miles, Langston and Jesse to see the path in front of them.

Worms, centipedes and other bugs traverse the walls. They move in and out of small holes like trains traveling through underground channels. Rats and other small rodents watch the group walk by, as they did their best to catch these same bugs for their supper.

The smell of soil and the natural gases it produced covers the air. The girth of the tunnels widen the further away the group travels from The Guardian's estate.

Langston is still forced to walk partially hunched over, up until the tunnel provides more room to stand. Miles and Jesse, on the other hand, hasn't any problem maneuvering in an upright position. Miles struts with his companions and snickers at how Langston appears.

"You humans - so impatient. Sheesh. I see nothing has changed since the last time I saw one of yous. Always in a hurry," he laughs quietly. "Are you happy now, cry-baby? *See*." Miles holds up his claw, directing Langston's attention to how the tunnels have expanded in from of them.

Langston, seemingly having spoken to soon, shrugs off Miles' comments in a moment of shame. He keeps walking.

"We dug like this to create a contingency," Miles adds.

"What you mean?" Langston jerks around.

"Contingency. You know what contingency means, right?"

"Uh . . ."

"If somebody, anybody - who don't belong in these here tunnels tries to come this way, we can force them into a bottleneck. Then, " Miles claps his claws, ". . . smash 'em."

Langston takes a moment to process the information. "Collapse the tunnels."

"Bingo. The smaller the tunnel, the easier to bring it down."

"Which way again?" asks Jesse, anxiously. He was only comfortable in the tunnels with which he was familiar. Visibly nervous, anxiety begins to take over his demeanor.

"Wait. We need to find out who this belongs to?" Langston holds up the gold pin that was once in Kinth's possession.

"Where did you get that?" Miles asks, sternly. He approaches Langston, reaching out for the pin. "I haven't seen one of those in years."

Langston quickly closes his hand. "When Kinth and I shook hands, he gave me this."

"Oh. Got it. I know someone who might know about that," Miles replies, walking away.

"Who?" Langston grabs Miles by his shoulder, jerking him in his direction.

"Easy on the fur, human. Let's just keep moving. We will deal with that later. Oh, and by the way; up here, we have a bit of a drop."

"What you mean 'a bit of a –'"

Langston loses his footing, falling on his backside before he can finish his question. Miles and his group of mole counterparts had created routes that included steep slopes which were divided into lanes. Slopes that were strategic drops, created to provide the necessary momentum. These aided the group in making it to the next section of tunnels quickly. Walking the route would have required time that the group didn't have to spare.

"Jesse - now you." Miles pushes Jesse before he has time to think, who follows down the drop behind

Langston in a parallel lane. The group slides down and around the route at great speeds.

"What the hell?!" Langston shouts. He tries to control how fast he is going, grabbing at the walls of his lane, but unsuccessfully.

"Just go with it, human. Stop trying to slow down! You have to make it across the gap! You-"

"I thought you said I shouldn't be in a hurry?!" Langston cries out, his voice cracking with fear. "What?! A gap?! Ah!"

"You will be fine! Trust me!"

"This is fun!" Jesse shouts. He enjoys a moment where he can be a kid, and not just a tool at Pearl's disposal. "Oh sh-!"

Eventually, the group comes to the end of the route: the gap. Miles and Jesse are launched into the air because of the speed they are traveling. They fall near each other and onto a dirt-covered platform, unwillingly smashing into one another.

Langston is launched into the air in a similar fashion, but falls short of this same area. "Ah! Help! Help!" He screams as he hangs from the edge. He looks below at his dangling legs and the darkness beneath his feet. The view below feels like a sinister creature breathing on him, especially because of the warm air that graces his skin. The air gradually wraps itself around him, feeling as if the creature is trying to slowly grab him by the bagginess of his pants to pull him downward.

"Don't look down, human. Nobody ever told you that. Focus on where ya tryin' to go, not what's behind ya. Don't look down." Miles coaches Langston from the platform, while waving Jesse and his companions over for assistance. "C'mon. Help me get this guy up before he pisses himself. We gotcha, human."

The group grunts and groans as they pull Langston up, enough where he can use his forearms to hoist himself atop the platform. Once safe, Langston lies on the ground out of breath, staring at a large stone that is positioned against a wall of dense soil.

"Good grief."

"Sorry 'bout that, human. Another *contingency*," Miles chuckles more.

"Whoa. Where are we?" Jesse's voice rises.

The light seems to glow, reflecting various colors from off the rocks and minerals. More light shows slightly through the cracks of the large stone.

"Shh. Keep it down, kid. Your human friend already made enough noise." Miles and his mole companions walk softly toward the stone. "We created a little nook for us to hide away in. When things get too heated inside the city or above ground - anywhere really - we come down here. I bring the family whatever they need. Nobody knows about this place, 'cept for us - and you twos now. We made a new tunnel to get to The Guardian's place, to get y'all."

The groups of moles pile against the stone in unison, moving it to the side almost effortlessly.

"Wow," Jesse whispers. "I didn't know it was more of you. I mean, like this many."

"Yep. I keep most of my family down here, and other small mammals like us. 'Cause jerks around that city like to catch us, kill us and sell us. This is our little safe haven. It's done us well so far."

"Sell you? To who?" Langston asks.

"To people. Anyone. Everyone. They skin us and use our fur. Have you felt how cold it can get sometimes out there? The climate is unpredictable and crazy. They need our fur to keep warm."

Jesse walks around the hidden environment, awed by its magnitude. His mouth is slightly open, as he touches the large stones encased in soil. *How did they create and hide a place this big?* he thinks.

Another mole walks smoothly toward the group as Miles explains the reasons for the nook. The slightly slender mole hands him a cup, to which Miles takes a sip of the contents.

"Mmm. Tasty. Want some?" He practically shoves the cup into Langston's face.

"What is that?"

"A specialty drink. A little water, earwigs, cockroaches – mmm. Looks like some crickets too." Miles stirs the drink with the tip of a nail on his claw. "Hey, babes. What else ya put in here?"

"I found ya some grasshoppers! The big ones you like. Do your friends want some?"

"My girl," Miles looks back at Langston. "And grasshoppers. She knows what I like." He slurps insect juice from off his claw.

Langston cringes, his stomach turning. "I'll pass. I'm good."

"Ya sure?"

Langston nods.

"Ah, well. Suit ya self." Miles takes another sip, and then wipes his mouth. ". . . Oh, and by the way – you need to rub some of that soil on ya. If we can smell ya, other things can smell that stench too."

"You talkin' 'bout the Desert Dwellers?"

"Eh, not quite. They don't come down here. They kinda hang around above ground, so I hear. We are deep down. Other stuff down here. We took a risk diggin' this deep. But it's the safest home base for us right now until we can find somewhere better. So yous good here."

"Well, how do you get around without alerting them?"

"By smell or when it's light out. That's when we try to dig. And dig fast. Those sand people tend to come out when it's dark. But don't hold me to that. Everything in these parts is unpredictable. We do our best to avoid 'em."

"What other stuff? What other stuff is down here?"

"You ask a lotta questions, don't you? Don't worry about it. We are good right now. Just rub the soil on you and follow directions. You'll be okay. Yous safe with me."

UHMANDRA

After staring at Miles for a moment, Langston grabs a large chunk of soil with one of his hands. He spreads it around into the other, while then wiping it on his face and clothing. "So . . . which way leads outta here? We need to go."

"What's the rush? Where you tryin' go? Besides, it's dark up there now. Can't risk it." Miles asserts himself as the keeper of light, above and underground.

"How you know it's dark? I thought that light comes when it wants? So how are we able to see down here?"

"I just do, human. Goodness." Miles jumps to his feet and paces the room. He scratches his head. "Listen – it's dark. I'm pretty sure. Okay? I can just feel it. Or it will be soon. We moles have senses that you don't. And yes, no one knows when the dark leaves or when light comes. But if you pay attention, you will start to get the pattern. You will start to feel it. Sometimes you can't just see with your eyes, human."

"Well, I'm not trying to stay down here. Maybe it will be light by the time we get to the surface." Langston begins to prep himself for a solo journey. He inspects the area, searching for the way back above ground.

"Yous hard of hearing, huh? I'm not risking it. *Capisce?*"

"I will go alone then. Just tell me which way I need to go."

"Ah, the tough guy again. Okay, tough guy – and go where?"

"Take me to who owns the pin. Maybe they know somethin.' They gotta know *something*!"

Miles jerks his head back, frustrated. "Sheesh. You and this pin again."

Find the Human

"Shaida-Pearl."

The Guardian sings Pearl's name as he enters the large, floral-designed bedroom; one of many rooms in the mansion. It's equipped with a high ceiling, crown molding and a tall and wide stone fireplace. Semi-naked, eccentric statues stand on the floor near the room's corners.

A sizable, tan bed with columns at its four points is positioned near a bay window. The glow from outdoors brightens part of the several throw pillows and a large comforter draped across it.

Pearl is smoking a slim cigarette while sitting on a chaise in front of the bed, gazing out the window. She switches between looking at her reflection in the glass, to looking at the lush floral garden with large bushes which was just feet away from the window.

"I swear, girl. What have you gotten yourself into? Hmm? Have I not given you all that you desired? All that you asked of me? All the food, drink and lines you ever needed?! All I asked of you in return is to control the riffraff. All I asked of you was to keep it out of my city." The Guardian forms a villainous smile. "Was that too much to ask?"

"It's *Madam Pearl* now. You know I don't go by that name no mo'." Pearl places her plump lips on the cigarette, taking a long pull. Smoke fills her lungs before she releases it through her nose. The smoke briefly covers her face. She speaks to her brother without looking his way, as if he is just a fixture in the room.

"Put that shit out. Right now. Ain't smoking in my place. Not in my house," The Guardian orders.

"This ain't yo' place."

The Guardian frowns. "Such a disgusting habit." He turns his attention to his security, snapping his fingers. "Gimme a minute."

The guards, wearing three-piece suits, leave the room. Two of them remain outside the doors. The Guardian sits in front of Pearl, after grabbing a chair that was once positioned by a vanity against the wall. He loosens his tie before speaking again, staring at Pearl the entire time.

"Do I really need to ask? Do I really need to say anything more?" He rubs his jawline as he speaks distinctly, forming a tight-lipped frown.

"What do you want, *Franklin*?"

"Oh, that's the response I get? No love for your brother? The one who has given you *all* that you ever wanted. The one who keeps you fed, despite the scarcity of real food around here. Really?" He pats Pearl on her leg. "It's been a while since we had a long, *loving* talk . . . *sis*."

"Hmph. Loving. You love nothing but yourself. And we never had problems with food until you–"

"Quiet!" The Guardian demands. "Don't be like this. Make this easy on ya self, Shaida-*Pee*."

"I *said* don't call me that!" Pearl exclaims, flicking her cigarette toward The Guardian, hoping to hit him with it. Instead, it lands at his feet. She knew what buttons of his to push, and he knew hers. Buttons that stand out like sore thumbs.

The Guardian frustratingly extinguishes the cigarette with the sole of his hard-bottomed, Oxford dress shoes before rushing Pearl. He then violently grabs her with both of his hands. One hand is positioned on her throat; the other maintains a grip at the root of her hair which is pulled back in a messy bun.

Pearl struggles to free herself from his grasp.

"WHERE DID THIS HUMAN COME FROM?! And why in the hell is he inside my city?! Inside my home?! Huh?! Huh?! Tell me what you know!" The Guardian screams while he removes his hand from Pearl's throat, reaching into his pocket. He pulls out the watch which he retrieved from Langston, nearly shoving it into Madam Pearl's face.

"I don't know, Franklin! I'm tellin' you the truth! I don't know anything! I don't know!"

The Guardian rubs his sister's cheek with the back of his fingers. His lips tighten more while his eyelids shudder. He swallows deeply before his hands begin to extend. His fingers combine and form into forelegs. His face changes, but not completely, transforming him partly into a Praying Mantis.

"Franklin, no! Stop! Please! *Please*!" Pearl yanks and kicks, but cannot break away from his grasp.

"What happened to us, Shai? Hmm? Where did we go wrong? Was it when we were kids?" His grasp gets tighter. The tibial spines in his forearm grow in length, just inches away from his sister's face. "Yes. I think it was. When you were. . . " The Guardian shoves her to the floor, ". . . given everything you wanted! And I was alienated!"

Madam Pearl screams in anguish as she hits the hardwood surface. The violent act scratches her face and bruises her arm; leaving marks that begin to heal slowly after they are inflicted. She holds her cheek and gathers her breath to respond to The Guardian's savageness. "You alienated yourself! You have always been spiteful! I hate you!"

"Shut up!" The Guardian, kneeling, grabs Pearl by her face again. "And tell me where this human came from, or I will snap your neck like a twig! Let's see how fast you heal from that!" The Guardian's face mutates between human form and that of the Mantis, like the flicker of a hologram. He hisses at her before repeating himself. "You betta' tell me something right now!"

Pearl shrieks again, "I don't know! I swear! My men brought that human to me. I don't know anything about him." She trembles, as her tears smear the makeup on her face. "You a horrible, horrible person! You swear you tough! But you ain't tough! Just a bully! Ain't no man! No man does this to a woman! Did you do this to your brother?! Huh?! I bet you won't try this with him! You scared of Kinth! That's right! Scared!"

The Guardian, with a straight-face, mutters under his breath as he lets go of Pearl. He reverts into his normal, human appearance as he stands upright. He sighs, wiping his hands on Pearl's blouse before walking away as he quickly remembers all of the fights they had as kids.

"One day, Pearl. One day. That tongue of yours – whew! One day. Don't think for one second that, just because you and I are blood . . . that I will treat you any different than those people outside the gates. You are only here to work, just like everyone else." The Guardian notices Pearl's running makeup, "You and all that filth on your face. You never saw momma wearing that shit. What are you hiding?" He makes his way to the door.

"To hell with you, Franklin! Something's wrong with you! And you did something to Daddy, didn't you?! Didn't you?! I know it!" Pearl screams.

The Guardian ignores her words. "Keep her in here. Looks like she will be our unwanted guest for a while. Let's go visit the other family in the cellar. Oh, what a joyous reunion this is! Where the hell is The Mantis when I need him?"

The Guardian slams the doors behind him as he exits the room. The locks on the door click, and the room is silent once more, except for Pearl's staggered breathing.

"You – find The Mantis. Get a status. When they find this human, tell The Mantis to bring him to me! Lock down all the exits! Do whatever you need to! Now! I knew I should have put an end to this ordeal when I had the chance."

Several streets away, the security threat level has been increased.

Meeee-orrrrr! Meeee-orrrr! Meeee-orrrr!

The booming, intense sound of the alarm continues to ring over braying screams and conversation. The city's citizens and visitors move briskly, some stumbling over one another in attempts to follow the orders delivered by The Guardian's security. Anxiousness and curiosity blanket the town.

"What is that?" asks Sam.

"Sounds like somethin' goin' on," Rahzy says, distinctly.

"Obviously, genius. But what?"

"Everybody outside! Now!" Guards equipped with HeatMods, paralyzers and energy rifles positioned themselves at all the exits. Others - holding shields - made their way to every table game, slot machine and lounge, clearing each venue of its patrons.

"Hit me," a short, chubby gambler orders. He has one large jagged, discolored skin boil on the side of his face. He has been gambling for quite some time, as well as drinking.

Before the dealer can deal another card, a guard pounds his paw on the felt hard enough to make the chips and cups of ale fly into the air, startling everyone at the table.

A tall, lanky fellow, with pale skin and gray eyes, complains to the guard about his act. The guard, in return, grabs him and puts him into a headlock, snapping his neck like a toothpick.

"Anyone else got something to say? Hmm?" the guard huffs. "Now move!"

"Sheesh," Rahzy mumbles to himself.

"Rah!" Sam snaps his fingers, "What's goin' on?" asks Sam.

"They say we gotta go."

"Go where?" Sam inquires.

"Outta here," Rahzy points with his thumb.

"Why?"

"Don't know. I was up three hundred lines, too. They killing my streak! My old lady is not goin' like it when I don't come home with the ends I promised her."

"But, wait. Why? We just got here!"

"Move, you two." Guards make their way into the conversation, shoving the gamblers in their backs.

The Mantis watches the unit works from one of the VIP sections in the distance. He reclines in one of the plush chairs, where he crosses his legs.

"Because there's a human somewhere," someone responds.

The two turn their attention to the new, easy-going voice which makes its way near.

"A human? Stop bullshittin'," replies Sam.

"It's true."

"Ha! Human. *Please*. People in this city have heard this human talk for a while," Rah interjects in disbelief. "Always nonsense."

"Why would I lie about this?"

The two shrug, almost in unison.

"Maybe it's somebody who *looks* human."

"There are plenty of people here who look human, but they always got something more up their sleeve. Wake up, Rah!" Sam replies, before turning his attention back to the new person who joined the conversation. "But, who are you? We don't know you."

"Have you ever seen a human yourself? With your own eyes?" the stranger asks.

A quiet falls amongst them despite the commotion.

"Exactly. I have. The name's Benard. People call me Benny."

"I'm Sam. This clueless being is Rahzy."

"Pleasure."

"So – talk, *Benny*." Sam jabs Benny in the chest with his finger.

"Um, yeah. So. . ." Benny wipes off his shirt in a slightly annoyed fashion. "My friends and I – we came to Hock to shoot the shit. Heard it was some good action out here. Heard that out of the seven corridors, this was the place to be. But anyway. On our way here, we heard people talking about a human."

"People? What people? Where?"

"Just people. I don't know who. Outside the walls. Out near Highway 99. Overheard somebody say that they saw a kid walking with some guy. This same kid and the guy were seen later, running from security. Somebody heard the word 'human' being tossed around."

Sam and Rahzy look at each other quickly, then look back at Benny.

"Ha! Get outta here! There is always somebody running from the security around here. People try to rob these spots – or each other - all the time! Dummies! This place is full of lowlifes and criminals!" Sam scoffs.

"Yeah – remember that case we had? What was his name? Lionel? Lenny? No – Leon! Yeah, Leon! This guy named Leon tried to steal and sneak goods out the city without export permission. Idiot," Rahzy adds.

"Right!"

"But what about them hearing the word 'human'?" asks Benny.

"They probably misheard."

"Well, regardless. Just telling you what I know."

"What you *think* you know," Sam skeptically chimes in, chuckling.

"Whatever. I don't miss much. Sounds like this place is worried about this human. The human who's here, but not here, if you catch my drift. Later." Benny waves his hand as he walks away toward the exit.

"You think he's tellin' the truth?" asks Rahzy.

Sam strokes his face. "Who cares?"

"But there could be a bounty on this human."

"I wants no part of a chase, especially involving a human. Ya understand me?"

"But what about our quota?" Rahzy asks.

Sam ponders. "You know, Rah, sometimes you can be very smart or very dumb. There is no in between with you."

"Go to hell, Sam."

Out of Reach

THE GROUP FEELS A RUMBLE AROUND THEM, as they travel the strategically designed tunnels. The type of rumble caused by deep and powerful thunder, which sometimes violently shakes the ground on which they walk.

Bits of soil and rock fall from the walls of the tunnels. It hit Langston, Miles and Jesse on different parts of their bodies before dropping to the ground.

Miles places his claw on one of the underground walls, becoming more unhappy with Langston's choice to keep going. The shakes have unnerved him.

"You really need to do this now?"

"Yeah. I do," Langston responds, curtly.

Miles sighs at Langston's response, as he makes his way to where his wife is sitting. She is relaxing in the middle of a small group of her adolescent offspring. The rest of the bunch are scattered around the space, playing or talking to each other.

"Babes, I gotta go."

"But you just got here," she replies wearily.

Miles rubs her shoulders gently. "I know. I know. But see, this human doesn't want to stay down here. Honestly, I don't blame him. This place is not meant for people like him," he whispers. "I'm going to take him close to the surface, but then I will be right back. Right back – I promise. I am not goin' with him. He is on his own after this. My job will be done. Okay? Sound good?"

Before Miles' wife could respond, he gives her a hug and kiss. Then, he makes his way toward Langston.

"Okay, guy. I am going to take you as far as I can go. You do realize that you are taking a risk going out there right now?"

"A risk I have taken before," Langston says, with uncertainty in his voice. He dusts himself off and stands assertively.

Miles moans with feelings of dismay. He shakes his head. "Just throwing caution to the wind, huh?"

"I will go, too." Jesse approaches them.

"No, kid. The human wants to do this on his own, so let him do this on his own."

"I agree with him, Jesse. You been a great help, but I can take it from here. At least for now. We will connect later once I figure things out." Langston speaks calmly, quickly reflecting on everything that has happened up until this point.

"I am not a kid! I'm sick of being babied! I can handle myself better than both of you! Why do you think I make runs for Madam Pearl?!"

"Kid - -"

"No! You can't stop me from coming! You leave me, and I will yell at the top of my lungs until you get back. See how those sand people like that. And whatever else is down here."

Jesse's face begins to slightly change in color.

"But you're not a baby, huh? You done? You finished?" Miles chuckles.

Jesse folds his arms and leans against the wall.

"Okay, kid. Let's go. But I'm done after this. You hear me? *Done.*"

Langston digs deep for a smile. He is slightly amused by Jesse's tantrum-filled enthusiasm. Jesse's demeanor reminds him of a younger version of himself. A time when he rebelled against his mother's desires, just to prove to that he was more mature than she believed.

He then begins silently pondering, while Miles and Jesse talk more about the journey ahead:

Why does everyone keep pointing out that I'm different? That I'm human? I can't be the only one like me around. Everyone in my city seems to look like me in a way. Definitely not like the people in Hock City. I mean, there are some crazy people in my city, but nothing like I've seen here, I guess. They seem normal back home, at least to me.

Like Talicia's crazy ass. Her and those bright red locks. Man, I love her hair. Why is her hair bright red, though? Probably just a style, I guess. But damn, her hair almost hangs to the floor. Who knows? And her eyes; those light, gorgeous eyes with those long lashes. Man. But there are other people with light eyes, right? I don't know.

Everything seems different; not what it seems anymore. I gotta get home. The only safe place I know.

Seems like a safe place to me. Momma never seemed too worried; she never took me beyond the walls, though. Why didn't she take me to another one of these cities when I was younger? She never told me about those other cities. Why not?

Miles abruptly pats Langston on the back, "Yo – human. You ready or what? Or did you change ya mind?"

"No. I'm ready."

"Well, then. Let's do this."

Back in the cold, dusty cellar, Kinth looks at the barrels of ale that blocks the hole that Miles created through which Langston and Jesse would escape. He wonders how far they have traveled. He also wonders why he is still where he is, when he has the intelligence and the strength to escape himself.

The quiet is all too normal to him, which is why he hasn't moved. He is used to solitude, staying mostly in the abandoned gas station in the outskirts of the Pines. He sings aloud and softly; one of the many things that keep his mind occupied.

Oh, it sho has been. . .

A mighty long time,

Since I journeyed,

With you on my mind.

At a fork in the road,

Not looking behind. . .

Searching for the truth,

That's been so hard to find...

He pretends to be bound to the column to which he had been chained before; before the change of events that took place in the cellar. He sits with his legs crossed on the floor, his head back resting on the post. He then lowers his voice and hums the rest of the tune as voices outside the doors get louder.

The locks on the cellar doors click before the knobs are turned, and the doors open. The light that shines into the room is interrupted by the movement of bodies entering the space; several individuals and many footsteps.

"Ah, my brother Kinth," The Guardian looks around as he speaks. "Wait. Wait a minute. I told you to bring them all to the cellar!"

"We did, sir." The Guardian's men are alert but nervous, scrambling for a response.

"Well, where are they? Find them!"

"They are long gone. Out of your reach, *brother*," Kinth interjects calmly.

"Nothing is out of my reach."

The Guardian snaps his fingers and twirls his hand. Security scours the cellar nervously, looking for Langston and Jesse. They know that The Guardian doesn't have much patience, so they need to find the two quickly.

They walk down each row in the room, checking under and in between the large barrels of ale. They check behind stacks of boxes and books in a back corner of the area. Storage closets on one side of the room are found empty.

"You won't find them here, brother." Kinth shouts before laughing.

"Shut your filthy, mouth!" The Guardian replies angrily. "Where is the Mantis?! I need him, now!"

"He is in the city, sir. Overseeing the evacuation."

The Guardian scoffs.

"Sir, they aren't here," another guard interrupts.

"Was the door guarded the entire time, as I ordered?"

"Yes, Guardian."

"Impossible! There is no other way out of this room," The Guardian speaks with rage, slamming his hand on a table violently.

"There is always other ways," Kinth interjects, calmly. He again begins to hum the song.

"Stop humming that stupid song! I've always hated that song!" The Guardian shouts. He grows aggravated, growling under his breath.

He begins to mutate into full Mantis-form in response to Kinth's comments. His arms stretch beyond his sleeves as his head becomes elongated and round. His eyes become bright green, bulging and widening inside of their sockets. His legs pierce through the seams of his pants, shifting his bones. The crunch sounds reflected tree limbs snapping.

He then stands in front of Kinth, grabbing his face aggressively. "Just like Father. I see that you have grown delicate with age, old man." The Guardian squeezes

Kinth's throat with force, but falls short in his efforts to inflict fear upon his brother.

"And you are still weak, just like the boy inside you. A boy . . . that never grew to be a man."

Kinth grunts before he head-butts The Guardian. He then forcefully rises to his feet, jerking his body to break free of his grasp. He brings his arms to the front of his body and lunges at his brother, following with a blow to his chest. He uses the chains in his hand for added vigor.

The Guardian grabs his head in agony. He cries out for help after he falls back against a nearby wall, changing uncontrollably between the human version of himself and a Mantis. Regaining his footing, he exchanges punches with Kinth. The two engage in close quarter combat: short fist-to-forearm, along with elbow-to-head blows. Leg sweeps and knee lunges.

The Guardian calls out again to his men after realizing that he is not winning the brawl. Security returns, swarming the center of the room and surrounding them both.

"Why are you standing there?! Don't just stand there looking stupid! Get him!"

The guards join in a full attack on Kinth from multiple angles, doing their best to subdue him as they did before during Kinth's journey to The Guardian's estate. They grab his legs and arms but can't hold onto him.

"Your men are weaklings like you, brother!" Kinth screams, between ducking and delivering bone-shattering blows. He tosses the smaller guards to the side like old rags.

"Net him!" another guard yells.

Kinth directs his attention to the voice behind the command. At this moment, a net flies through the air from the same direction, after a sharp swoop sound from the barrel of a gun.

Kinth raises his hands to grab the net in midair, thinking he would tear or quickly dismantle it. But this was no ordinary netting. He begins to shake uncontrollably as his hands grip the metal-linked roping. He trembles before falling to his knees and collapses face down. Saliva pours from the side of his mouth as he lay on the ground. His skin becomes flush as the roots of his white beard are fried.

The Guardian gathers himself and walks toward his momentarily motionless brother. He reforms completely into the human version of himself, his shredded clothing hanging from his limbs. Adjusting his arms back in place, he forcefully blows blood from his nostrils onto the floor.

"Look what you made me do to my suit! It took a lot of time to make this! You brute! You and that sister of yours. For the life of me. . ." He paces around Kinth's body, groaning at his loss of fine menswear and the bodily abuse he attained. He kicks Kinth before speaking again. "That was neuro-netting, brother. What you are feeling is the equivalent of a stroke inhabiting your body. Your nervous system has been hijacked." He lets out an unruly laugh. "Even with all your muscles and your measly strength – your power is no match for this. I had it designed specifically for people like you. Impressive, right?"

Kinth shudders as he lay on the floor. His breathing is heavy. He can barely move his fingers, or any other part of his body, except for his eyes and his mouth. He stares at The Guardian out of one eye.

"I knew you would return, brother," The Guardian adds. "And I was ready for you."

Kinth swallows deeply before replying, "F – F - Fuck you, Franklin."

The New Normal

MILES CONTEMPLATES BREAKING THE MONOTONOUS MINUTES OF SILENCE, as the group comes closer to the tunnel's exit.

The quiet has been killing him, understandably so. He was used to either the noise of the city – Madam Pearl and her boisterous orders and laughter - or the noise of his large family. He was additionally used to talking a lot to anyone. But for the moment, the only noise present was the sounds of footsteps, along with wind and the mild chatter of the unknown around them.

"Keep up, you two. Not too much further." He sniffs the air and touches the walls. "So, human. . ." he continues, scratching at his fur. ". . . You goin' tell us where ya from or what? Inquiring minds want to know."

He keeps a steady pace forward, speaking to Langston without turning his attention to him completely. He is focused and determined to do what he promised his wife he would, so that he could return to her and his family safely.

Jesse walks with his head down, listening to Miles question Langston about things which he wanted to know the answer to himself. And the subtle sounds of the tunnel environment: the light hum of locusts, the mating call of crickets and the wind that howls above ground. A howl that somehow also echoes below the surface.

"It's the least you could - -"

"Longleaf. I'm from Longleaf," Langston interrupts Miles before he could grill him further.

Miles stops suddenly and stares at Langston; studying his eyes to find the truth. "Get outta here," Miles waves his hand in disbelief. "That place is almost as bad as Hock. No humans out there. You would be dead already."

"Why would he be dead?" asks Jesse, inquisitively.

Miles sighs, "When Pineville changed, over time humans became frowned on. *They* became the different ones; the minorities. We — us; people like me and you, kid. We are the new normal. Humans were taken away and sent out to die. Thrown to the wild things that lurk out here. Understand? You follow what I'm sayin'? The other people separated and went their own way. Made new lives for themselves."

Jesse tries to makes sense of what was said. His face grows covered with gloom, as if he was one of the humans who were sent away.

"Wait. So, Jesse – you have abilities, too?"

Miles stops again. "Hold up! Hold up! *Hold* up! You been with this human all this time and you didn't show him what you could do? C'mon, kid. Show him!"

"Nah, I don't want to."

"Why not?"

"I just don't want to!" Jesse's voice rises.

"Okay, okay. Goodness. Don't blow a gasket. But yeah, he does have abilities. But not everyone does. Some people weren't as fortunate as the kid. Most got sick; eventually died. Some others grew extra arms and fingers. Eyes, tongues, etc. Morbid shit. The others - well; these people ignore their abilities, or hide them."

"Hide them? Why?"

"I don't know. So they won't expose what they can do, I guess," Miles shrugs. "Some abilities can be used for the wrong things. But anyway. There is something odd about this. I'm actually shocked to hear you are from Longleaf. But, whatever." He scoffs before he starts to walk again. "Okay, right up there is the exit. A slab of wood is up there over the hole. Give it a good whack. You should be able to move it to climb out. When you get above ground, just follow the path. It should lead you to some houses."

"Which house?" asks Langston, wiping his face of debris to see better.

"The house will find you. I'm outta here."

"You're not comin'?"

"That's a negative, kid. My work is done." Miles extends his fist to Jesse, to which Jesse slowly extends his fist in return. They give each other dap before parting ways. "Well, 'Human from *Longleaf*,' safe travels."

"Yeah. Thanks. You are okay, Miles. Bit of an ass, but okay."

"Yeah, well. You can't spell assertive without an ass. You don't survive in these parts being nice all the time or by asking so many damn questions. Just relax and observe where possible. One of these days you will learn how to do this."

Jesse pushes on the slab of wood while Langston and Miles share odd pleasantries. Wood chips and dust falls in his face as he slides it. He is shocked that he can move the wood on his own.

"That was easy," he thinks aloud.

"Yeah. We don't make our exit points too hard to get out of. Around here, sometimes you gotta move in a hurry." Miles turns to walk away. "I'm outta here. See ya."

The sky begins to show as Langston moves the wood more. He moves his face from behind the shadow of the slab of lumber, and it becomes illuminated from the sky's gradient glow. The glow is a mixture of dark purple with red highlights. Specs of white are scattered about resembling stars.

Unlike Miles' prediction, it was neither dark above ground at this time, but neither was it light. The sky's glow was dark enough to exude the last few minutes of a sunset, but light enough to see some of the surroundings. The area is lit enough whereas Langston feels he didn't have to worry about the things that moved in the shadows.

"Hold on. Let me go out and look around."

"I'm coming, too," Jesse insists.

Langston presses his lips at Jesse's stubbornness, but agrees. He and Jesse ease out the tunnel opening, inspecting the area. The wind picks up, blowing the tall grass and tree branches. The neon lights of Hock City shine from the south. The stir of the wind makes Jesse nervous, causing the color of his skin to flicker.

"So, are you going to tell me how you do that?"

"Do what?" replies Jesse, hesitantly.

"That." Langston nods his head downward. The color of Jesse's hands changes slightly to match the grass they walk through. "I can't believe I'm just noticing that," Langston continues.

"I don't know. I just — I just do it."

"Damn. That's amazing. That's how you survive out here, isn't it? It's gotta be the only way you can move through this craziness," Langston asserts.

"I guess. It's hard for me to control. Especially when I'm —"

"When you're nervous . . ."

"Yeah, I guess. I'm still learning how to control it."

Langston stops and admires Jesse's ability for a moment. The two then gradually make their way down the road, hoping to find the home of which Miles spoke. As they continue to walk, various paths appear but then disappear, as they blend in with the foliage. One of the paths remains, but splits between a trail to the backdoor. Another trail for the side door is also connected to the front of the house. The confusing thing for Langston and Jesse is that all sides of the house look the same.

"Which way?"

"I – I don't know." Langston looks ahead closely.

"What's that noise?"

A faint sound repeats itself every few seconds, causing the two to become alarmed and stand perfectly still. Langston looks back at the lights behind him, wondering what was happening in the city since he and Jesse escaped.

Back in Hock, the city streets are like a meatpacking plant outside of the Line District. Thousands of people seem smashed together like sardines, while they are being forced outside of the main gate.

"You don't have to shove us! You don't treat visitors like this!" Sam screams.

"Yeah! You freakin' jerk!" Rah co-signs Sammy's argument.

"Now what?"

"No point staying around here," Sammy says, looking around.

"So? Find the human? The quota?" asks Rah. His excitement causes his wings to involuntarily flutter.

"Ah, quota-schmota!"

Rahzy ignores Sammy's comment. Approaching a nearby guard, he grabs his arm abruptly.

"Yo, I know where the human is."

The guard, amid moving people outside the gates, stops suddenly. He lets out a visible huff before turning around. His eyes widen as he puts his index finger in front of his mouth, seizing Rah by his shirt with his other hand.

"Shh. Quiet down. What *human*?!"

"Don't b-s me, dude. I know about the human. And we can find 'em." Rahzy jerks away.

"What are you doing, Rah?! Don't tell him that," whispers Sammy, pulling Rah further away from the guard. "We don't know if what that guy said is true. We don't know him from Adam."

"Doesn't matter. I believe him. Besides, we need the lines, man. Chill. Relax. I got this. Aren't we bounty hunters?"

Sam sighs.

"So, let's hunt . . . and get this bounty. We came here looking for violators, right?" Rahzy's eyebrows raise like his wings.

Sam crosses his arms and taps one of his feet, looking around in a disconcerted fashion. He rubs his brow, mumbling to himself for a short time. Then, he waves his hand at Rahzy in hesitant agreeance. Rahzy turns his attention back to the guard.

"Stay right there," the guard orders while in stride.

"Oh boy," Sammy murmurs. "Here we go."

"Relax, Sam." Rahzy says confidently, as he straightens out the wrinkled portion of his shirt.

Moments later, the guard returns with two of his larger counterparts. The group approaches Sam and Rahzy from behind, while the two stand and observe all the uproar around them. The guards grab both by their arms and heave them aggressively out of the venue.

"Mention a word about what you *think you know,* and we won't be as nice! Take them outside the walls with the others," the guard shouts from the doorway with a deep voice. He crosses his arms, smirking as Sam dusts himself off.

Rahzy hovers in the air, wings flapping. "Assholes! We know where the exit is!"

"Easy, Rah. Easy." Sam calms Rahzy as much as he can. "No need to get aggressive right now. That will expose why we are here. So . . . you said you want to get the bounty. Right? So let's get it. We don't need their permission."

"What you got in mind?"

Sam takes a moment to watch the activity before responding. "We'll talk outside the gates."

Just the Beginning

LANGSTON AND JESSE QUIETLY MOVE TOWARD THE HOUSE. The dwelling's design changes gradually, with each set of steps that brings them closer. First the shape of the windows change, then the curve of the back steps and doorways. The home seems to be fluid, moving in response to any nearby noise or movement.

"Whoa! What's happening?"

"I don't know," replies Langston. "You see that, too?"

"Yeah. That's crazy."

"Stay close," Langston cautiously moves forward.

UHMANDRA

The house continues to shift - bending, stretching and sometimes slowly spinning. Langston and Jesse became drawn to these movements.

"You are on private property!" a voice groggily shouts. "Please exit the premises!"

Jesse stands still, slightly drifting from side to side in a mild daze. He appears shocked, which is evident as his mouth hangs ajar. Langston tries to investigate, often shaking his head while attempting to figure out what is happening. While he feels coherent, at the same time he feels partially hypnotized as if he is watching himself from another dimension; some sort of out-of-body experience.

Say something. Tell 'em why you're here, he thinks. "Uh. Uh. We were told you could help us." Langston stammers. He looks up into the air, unsure on where to direct his words. It was as if the person behind the voice was sitting somewhere in the sky, or on the house's roof.

The house abruptly stops moving, reverting into its normal state. The sudden stop brings a gush of wind through the area, causing everything to suddenly move in slow motion.

"Hello?" Jesse carefully speaks, while looking around in wonder.

"I can't help you. Now go away!" the groggy voice speaks again.

"Why not?" Jesse asks.

"We don't need much. Just looking for an answer to one question," Langston adds. "Just one question."

"I got lines I can share!" Jesse adds. "Well, a little left, I guess." He mumbles further, tapping his arm.

"No thank you," the voice replies.

The house starts to morph into a face. The molding above and below the windows becomes wrinkled as it forms into elderly eyes and eyelids. The chimney mutates into a slightly crooked nose, as the strips of aged siding become lips and eyebrows.

Jesse, stepping away in awe of the changes, falls clumsily backward onto the ground. Langston moves to him and swiftly helps him up. He then stands in front of the home once more, but this time with more confidence.

"Please, just one question," Langston says again.

"One question?" the voice asks.

"Yes. One."

"I don't believe you! If you came from that city, you aren't to be trusted!"

The home spins quickly. The eyes blink.

"Really! One! Just one!"

"What do I get in return for my answer?"

Langston reaches into his pocket. "Is this enough?" he asks, holding his hand out with the pin resting in his palm.

Suddenly, Langston and Jesse become more coherent than what they were. After refocusing, they realize the area looks normal again, including the house. They were no longer on the path outdoors. Instead, they were in the home's foyer.

The strange voice speaks to them again. "I knew he would do as I asked."

"Hello?" Langston calls out, but the voice doesn't respond. "He, who?" he inquires.

"The person to who I loaned my pin."

"And who was that?" asks Langston.

"Ah! But you said one question!"

"Wait! I haven't asked my question yet."

"Oh, but you did! And I gave you one answer. I did as I agreed!"

"Hey! That's not fair!" interjects Jesse. He balls both of his fists in anger. Langston puts his hand on Jesse's shoulder to calm him.

The two move around inquisitively as they speak more, trying to figure out where the person behind the voice was hiding. He still hasn't shown himself.

"What's fair when the answers are already there?" the voice asks.

"Huh?" replies Jesse. "What the hell does –"

Langston covers Jesse's mouth, "Please, sir. Come out and be reasonable. Can we talk in person? We are desperate. Just one or two more questions. Please."

"I think I have been more than reasonable. Besides, I can speak to you from where I am."

"Don't you want your pin back?" Jesse asks. The tense emotion in his voice begins to fade.

"Leave it on the desk by the door."

The house changes again. Suddenly, Langston and Jesse are positioned closer to the main entrance than before. They grow woozier with each change of the environment.

"Can you stop that, please? Whatever it is you're doing?" Langston pleads, resting his hand against his head.

There is no response from the voice. Langston thinks hard during the moment of silence. Looking down at the pin, he shuffles it in his palm. Based on his response, he realizes that the man behind the voice knew about the pin, including who had it.

"They got Kinth. The Guardian. He got him. Don't know what's goin' to happen to him. I tried to get him to come with us, but he wouldn't come."

The environment changes again. This time, Langston and Jesse find themselves standing in a library, surrounded by piles of books. They are standing before a desk with a chair behind it. The back of the chair faces them - with a subtle stream of smoke rising from it into the air. The chair abruptly spins around.

"And what do you suppose I do about this? Hmm?" The elderly man speaks, taking puffs of his pipe. He blows more smoke - that forms into tiny, random objects into the air: A Trillium flower, a star, a tree and more. "Why do you think I can help you?"

Langston waves away the smelly cloud as he cautiously studies the man's face. He sits in one of the nearby chairs. "I don't know. I just figured you should know, since this is your pin and all." Langston puts the pin on the edge of the desk. "You gave it to him, right? I'm just looking for a way home that doesn't include being held captive, being killed or whatever. I don't like being threatened. Nor having my mind messed with like this. Kinth gave me this pin, because he knew it would find its way back to you, I think."

The elderly man continues to puff on his pipe without breaking the emotionless expression on his face.

Langston then leans forward, pointing his index finger at the desk. "Look. You have your pin back. And I told you about Kinth. Can you give me somethin'? Anything?"

The elderly man exhales deeply before taking another puff. He then responds, letting out a mouthful of smoke. "You look quite the mess. You have traveled a long way, have you?"

"Mmm hmm," Langston nods.

"Long way from - Longleaf, is it?" the elderly man adds.

"How did you know that?"

"Because I listen."

"But I haven't told you where I am from."

"Sometimes words are not needed to relay what needs to be said," the elderly man chuckles.

"Hey, how did we get in here? How did your house do that?" interjects Jesse. He studies the room, trying to examine everything quickly. "Was that like . . . magic?"

"He has abilities, too," Langston answers.

"So, you have been exposed to the likes of that city, I see. Everything it has to offer. . ." The elderly man leans forward.

"I have. Well, not everything. But what I have been exposed to was enough."

"What can you do?" asks Jesse.

"The better question is . . . what can *you* do? And why are you not doing it somewhere else?!" The elderly man counters with emphasis, pointing his pipe in Jesse's direction.

"I can't do anything," Jesse immediately gets quiet, looking down into his lap.

"I don't have time for this. Jesse, let's get outta here."

Langston jumps to his feet, making his way towards the library's door. The door disappears as he reaches for the doorknob, revealing nothing more than a wall. When he turns around, the chair in which he had been sitting has been repositioned in front of him, just inches away from where he was standing.

"Impatience is the killer of time, and time is precious. Use it wisely," says the elderly man. He extends his hand, pointing to the chair.

Langston reluctantly grabs the chair, bringing it back near the desk. He sits as Jesse wearily watches.

"Yes, I too have abilities," the elderly man decides to finally answer.

"Like?"

"I have the means to alter senses, amongst other things."

"What you mean?" asks Langston.

"Your senses. You have five senses, correct? Odd question for this place, but - I can make you see what isn't there, for example. Or change and modify what *is* there."

"Like the house. All the stuff you did to it."

"Yes."

"But how did we get in here? Inside?" Jesse chimes in.

"Oh, that was simple. I made you see other things before luring you inside. I preoccupied your mind to distract and entice you."

"Wow."

"But how did you know that I was from Longleaf?"

"Lucky guess," the elderly man jokingly responds, smiling.

"Bullshit," Jesse asserts under his breath.

The elderly man slams his hand down on his desk.

"*Jesse*," Langston frowns.

"Sorry."

"Now that we have *that* . . . out of the way, tell me who you are," says the elderly man, rubbing his now aching hand.

"My name . . . my name is Langston. I -," Langston clears his throat. "I know this is going to sound a little crazy, but I woke up in the middle of nowhere. Somewhere out in these fields, not too far away from Hock City. Jesse found me."

"Yeah. I was out looking for stuff – near 99. He was just lying out there," Jesse interjects. "I saved him."

"We walked a ways. I stumbled on Kinth at a gas station, not far from where Jesse found me. He wasn't much of a help at first. All he said was that people had been by his station before. He showed me some book with people's information in it or something. I left the station and figured I would get answers on my own."

"And how has this journey been, thus far?"

"I'm alive," Langston shakes his head.

"Ha! Indeed! But is being alive enough?" the elderly man asks excitedly.

"Uh –"

"Some questions don't need immediate answers. Please, continue."

"I'm alive, but barely. Those sand people – Desert Dwellers or whatever – nearly killed me. Kinth saved my life, though. Then Jesse helped me into the city," Langston adds, while he glances at Jesse over his shoulder. "That place is a madhouse. The people there – man! I met Madam Pearl. She is a piece of work. Between her and The Guardian - and those sand people - my life has been threatened more times than I can count. I just can't believe I am related to them."

"Related to whom?"

"Them. Kinth; Pearl; The Guardian. They are my siblings. At least that's what I was told."

"I see. Continue."

"That's it."

"No! That's just the beginning!" The man stands, crossing his arms behind his back. He walks to the nearest window, looking out at the land that surrounds his home. "How did you know to come here?"

"My boy Miles told us. He helped us," Jesse says.

"It's good to have friends. Yes?"

"I guess so. Can we call you a friend?" Langston asks.

"I believe I can help you get back to Longleaf."

"How? Tell me. Please."

"I can tell you, but you have to do something for me once you get there."

"Anything."

"Do I have your word on this?" the man extends his hand.

"Yes." Langston shakes his hand in agreement.

"Find a member of the Longleaf Counsel. Show them that pin. Tell them that the person who owns that pin would like to be a member of the city."

"How am I supposed to know who is on the counsel?"

"The same way you found me."

"But, why can't you go and say this yourself? Why do you need me? Why would they listen --"

"You sound so much like Kinth." The elderly man chuckles. "Longleaf is a special place. If you are truly from there as you say, you will have no issues with my request. Have faith in yourself."

"How do you know I will keep my word when I get there?"

"We are friends now, yes? Didn't we shake on it? Don't friends keep their word?"

Langston picks up the pin, once again shuffling it in his palm. He looks at it closely. "Yeah. Okay. So which way? Which way gets me home?" When he looks up, the elderly man is gone. The chair on which he had been sitting is empty. Only a small cloud of smoke covers the area.

"It's time for me to rest," the elderly man replies.

"But wait! Which way to home?!"

"Start where you ended." The man's voice rings throughout the home like an echo from a church choir. Moments later, without notice, Langston and Jesse are standing outside.

"What does that mean? Start where you ended?" asks Jesse.

Start where I ended. Start where I ended, Langston repeats the phrase to himself. Zoning out, he tries to make sense of the man's words.

"Mr. Langston?"

"I guess it means we keep going."

"Huh?"

"We pick up where we left off."

"Um, okay." Jesse sighs as he sits on the steps. He folds his arms and rests them across his legs. "I'm hungry."

Langston nods. Looking up toward the home, he bites his tongue with even more questions brewing in his mind. "Can we get something to eat? Drink? We are starving and tired."

The surroundings get quiet. The steady whistle of the wind calms. Suddenly, Langston and Jesse become lightheaded again. They are under the elderly man's powers once more, but briefly. Thereafter, a small loaf of bread, a bag of stale chips and two water bottles appear on the steps inside of an old milk crate. Two blankets are neatly folded nearby.

"Yes!" Jesse exclaims at the sight of something that would fill his stomach.

"Appreciate it!"

The two kick back on the front stoop of the home and enjoy a moment to rest.

Some Tears Can Be Fixed

PEARL SNORES LOUDLY, AT TIMES GASPING FOR AIR. Her large, solid frame moves like a bear in hibernation, as she inhales and exhales slowly. She has drifted into a deep sleep, with the butt of a lighted slim cigarette within the clasp of her fingers.

Her head is cocked back. One of her legs stretches down the slight curve of the chaise design upon which she rests. The aging chaise creaks with each deep breath she takes.

She awakens for a moment, when the sound of her own snoring startles her. Her heart races as she gathers herself. Wiping her eyes while breathing heavily, she realizes that the cigarette was burning the tips of her fingers.

"Ouch! Shit!"

Wiping her face with her alternate hand, she presses the remaining portion of the cigarette down into an ashtray. While extinguishing the cigarette, she looks at her reflection in the unstained part of the ashtray glass. She becomes disgusted at what she sees, launching the ashtray through the window of which she had been gazing out, just before she had fallen asleep. She then leans forward, resting her elbows on her knees. Pearl cries into her hands uncontrollably.

Suddenly, a ruffling sound can be heard which is followed by the faint sounds of grunts. "Pearl," a soft, familiar voice travels through the window. "You know, I always thought you'd be stronger than this."

Pearl looks up eagerly. Her tears smear the last bit of makeup she had on her face. "Miles?!"

"Shh. Yeah."

Miles stands on a ledge just outside of the window, speaking through the hole which Pearl created.

"What are you doing in here? Is he keeping you locked in here?"

Pearl scoffs, "Of course he is. How did you know I was here?"

"The kid told me you were here. Took some doing to find you up here, though. Couldn't catch your scent at first," Miles nods his head. "C'mon. Let's get you outta here."

Pearl shakes her head, sighing before standing and coming closer to the window to raise it. "My sweet Jesse. Is he okay?" Pearl rubs her brow, brushing off her moment of weakness.

"Yeah. He's with that human."

"With him where? Still downstairs?" Pear replies, nervously. "Oh no."

"No, no. We got them out."

"And Kinth?"

"I guess he is still down there. He wouldn't come with us. Actually, he couldn't come." Miles tries to look over Pearl's shoulder. "Can we go? I can tell you all this once you are outta here."

"I can't leave here. That asshole will find me within minutes." Pearl's voice rises an octave. She fumbles through her cigarettes angrily, trying to light another.

"Shh. I know his men are right outside the door."

"AH! FUCK HIM!" Pearl screams in disgust. She extends her middle finger toward the door. "Besides, go where?"

"To your uncle's."

Pearl chuckles faintly before sitting again, "Now I know you insane. That man wants no parts of this place, especially me and my good-for-nothing brother."

"Pearl – "

"And what's this I hear about Dad?"

"What?"

"Don't bullshit me, Miles."

"I'm lost over here. What about your father? What you talkin' 'bout?"

"Franklin has been telling us lies, Miles. At least that's what Kinth said."

"Well of course he has. But I promise you – I'm clueless on what you talkin' 'bout."

"Jerk. Just a . . . he has always been a jerk."

Miles disappointedly watches on as Pearl struggles with her emotions. He carefully extends one leg at a time through the window's opening. Sitting down gently on the pane, he looks at the floor to collect his thoughts before speaking again.

"You know, I always considered the three of yous like my own kids. I felt like – like I was an uncle to you myself. An unorthodox family of sorts. Your father could have killed me long before that stuff appeared in the sky. I was an annoyance to him, but he saw deeper. He realized that something bigger was goin' on. He saw me for more than the animal I am. He was in tune with nature. I was just trying to feed and provide for my family. Just like he was.

"And when things changed, and I could communicate with y 'all, we talked like brothers. I mean, after we got beyond the obvious shock and amazement, of course. He didn't want anything to do with me at first. Who would, right? A talking mole? Get outta here!" Miles chuckles. "I guess . . . what I am trying to say here is, I have known you since you were young. All three of yous. Sometimes families go through things that tear them apart. But some tears can be fixed. You know? Like stitched back together. Does that make sense? But you can't start to fix things if you stay here."

Pearl shakes her head, mumbling something to herself before she responds. "I'm tired, Miles. I'm exhausted. Like mentally. I can't do this place anymore."

"So, let's go then!"

"I can't. I'm slow. Look at me. I don't heal like I used to. My body different. I'm fat. I feel like – like . . . I'm getting old," Pearl replies. "Besides, he has had plenty of chances to kill me here. And he hasn't. If I leave –"

"He's not going to do anything to you," Miles interjects. "He's not. Never!"

"How are you so sure?"

"Cause he has been the same way since he was kid! He has always talked a big game, but never backed it up. He is just lost now; a confused soul. Misguided. But he still cares for both of you deep down. The problem is . . . he is unstable. He needs help."

"Well, that ain't nothin' new, Miles! I think he killed Daddy!"

"What?! Noooo!" Miles waves his claws in disbelief.

"Yes! And that human – somethin' is goin' on!"

"Pearl, please – c'mon. Let's get outta here. We can continue this talk later. I got a friend who can hide you in his potato cart. He can get you outside the walls. It won't be a comfortable ride, but a ride none the less."

One of The Guardian's suit-wearing henchmen hears the muffled conversation. He rushes the room with support from his counterparts.

"What's going on in here?!" one of the men shouts.

Another notices Miles and sprints towards the center of the room. He throws a flat, metal object toward the window. The object explodes, sending several small bits of jagged, metal-like daggers into the air toward where Miles is standing.

"Miles, go!" Pearl screams, just before one of the daggers hits him in the arm. "Miles!"

Miles grabs his arm with his opposite claw, just before falling out of the second story window. He falls into bushes where his companions notice and act quickly. They grab him, jetting to a nearby lump in the yard.

Pearl runs to the window, looking out of it briefly before being grabbed by the guards. They pull her arms behind her as they force her out of the room.

"What do we do with her?" asked one guard to the other.

"Take her to the cellar. Can't trust her in here by herself. And find that rat!"

What Kind of Commotion?

THE EXCHANGE IS BUSIER THAN USUAL. On most days, when a little peace makes its way near, everyone in this part of the Pines journeys to the market to barter goods. Or, often they just browse. It is a good way to pass the time when boredom of looking at Hock City's walls, or the miles of desert around it, settles in. Most just wanted to get out and do something: sick of looking at similar, discontent faces.

Sometimes it is a means to avoid random acts of violence which made its way through the towns like a passing storm. Being around a crowd of people was oftentimes safer than being alone. But today it was over-crowded, because of the recent events inside Hock.

UHMANDRA

Eli is one of the many people in the crowd. He pays his stand fee - today it is four bottled waters. And, it's not long before the swarm of people arrives. A fee is required to position his goods at the Exchange, so that these items could be visible on the market's main street; a payment method that was quite different than the lines used inside the city.

Most people outside of the walls relied on bartered goods. Drinkable water was the most popular; passes or lines into the city - second. And clothing is third; whatever is most important to the patron at the time. You just never know what you may need in these parts.

To be a part of the line system requires connections with city officials which the average public doesn't have, including Eli. It involves connections to the underworld with which he chooses not to associate. The people in the Pines were enough.

At various intervals, Eli straightens and dusts off his goods that he displays on an aged magazine display. His display is situated between Johnny on one side - a slightly older, thin man who was missing one arm; a connoisseur of wood carvings - and Sally on the other side. She works in repurposing. She takes the remains of old clothing, creating new fabrics out of the scraps. She constructs long, thick garments which the locals seem to love.

"Peace and light. Good luck today, Eli," Johnny says with his back turned, as he pulls his latest crafts from a stained plastic bin. Birds, rabbits, snakes and more – all carved out of wood.

"Peace and light. Likewise, J. I like the new additions you got there. Might have to grab one of your new ones for the wife."

"Appreciate it. Took me a little longer on these. My raggedy arm wouldn't cooperate this go 'round," replies Johnny. He laughs at his own self-deprecating humor. "I just hope I get rid of a couple. Not too many need stuff like this."

"You will. You will," Eli responds softly.

"I really need a sale today. Think we goin' do well? I hope these people come to buy," Sally chimes in. She has no eyes, seeing only by her other senses. She folds her clothes neatly.

"Let's hope so," Johnny replies.

As Eli works to keep his area clean, those passing by sporadically review his items. Most are exceedingly cautious in making any transactions, ensuring they are acquiring necessities versus things that just make them feel good. They do not know when they will have anything to trade again. Other times, the goods are inoperable and don't meet their needs.

"Hello, Mr. Eli!"

"Well, well, well. Look who decided to join us! Greetings, Ms. Mabel!" Eli responds, enthused to see another friend, and potentially make a sale or trade.

"What you got for an old lady?"

"Its 'bout time I saw yo' pretty face! Didn't think you were coming out today!"

"Oh, stop it. You sweet-talker."

"But uh – I don't have much this time, Ms. Mabel. The misses has the only thing I found that you might've liked, while I was north. I will be sure to keep you on my mind next time," replied Eli, apologetically.

"I sho'd appreciate that. Please do."

"Take a look at Ms. Sally's and Johnny's table. They have some nice, new items."

"I sho will," Ms. Mabel walks away. "Peace and light to y'all."

Eli and Johnny wave almost in unison to Ms. Mabel.

"I heard your boy saw some crazy stuff the other night," Johnny randomly says, sitting down in a wooden rocker behind his goods. "Out there by the highway."

"Is that — is that right?" Eli stammers.

As he and Johnny continue this new conversation, the bounty hunters - Sam and Rahzy - were not far away. They speak amongst themselves, pretending to be locals as they listen to various conversations. They hope to get any clues on the human from Hock.

"Not sure about any of that," Eli continues, intrigued by Johnny's statement.

"Yeah. Gracie's kid. She was telling us what Junior saw. Something about a fight out yonder." Johnny points toward the open desert flatland; the area just outside of the Exchange and surrounding homes.

Sam taps Rahzy's shoulder. At this moment, he's alerting him to Eli's and Johnny's conversation. The two gradually make their way over, doing their best to not be seen.

Dammit, Junior, Eli thinks. "Oh, oh — that. It was nothing. Just some, um - commotion in the fields." Eli reflects on his transaction with the man while north of Hock. His stomach suddenly feels like someone had opened a shaken soda can inside of it.

"Oh, okay. Just wanted to make sure he was good. It can be crazy 'round these parts. But you know that."

"Yes, sir! He's fine. Thanks."

"Commotion? What kind of commotion?" Sam asks, appearing behind Eli.

Eli – distracted - tends to his goods until he feels Sam's presence nearby. Rahzy aggressively sits down in Eli's chair that's positioned adjacent to his goods.

"Can I help you, uh - gentlemen?" replies Eli, looking at both visitors with apprehensive eyes. He concentrates on the two, ensuring he has one of them in his peripheral when speaking to the other.

"Tell us about this . . . *commotion*," Sam says.

"If you aren't buying anything, keep it moving," interjects Johnny, standing to his feet. "You –"

Before Johnny can finish his statement, Rahzy points a tan-colored, camouflaged handgun at Johnny's groin. "Sit down, cripple . . .," he says, motioning the gun downward. ". . . before you lose another limb."

Sam watches on, chuckling at Rahzy's intimidation tactic. "Now - back to you, sir. Commotion? Care to elaborate?" Sam rubs his palms together in a menacing fashion.

Eli uses the opportunity Johnny created to pull out the shotgun – the one he bartered from the large man up north. He points it directly at Sam's face. People scatter from the area in various directions. Ms. Sally ducks down and Ms. Mabel waddles away, petrified.

"I am just a humble businessman. Just looking to do my business and go home. Please, walk away." Eli was no stranger to violence and self-defense. Despite his stomach tightening, he spoke coolly while showing little to no nervousness.

"Would you look at this guy, Rah? The size of the balls on him. I'm impressed," Sam says. He speaks to Rahzy without breaking eye contact with Eli. "It's too bad."

"Yeah, it is," replies Rahzy, almost robotic.

"Too bad, for what?" asks Eli. He tries to glance over his arm at Rahzy, but doesn't do this fast enough. While he is distracted, Sam grabs the shotgun by the barrel, yanking it from Eli's grip. Sam then flips it so that the handle is positioned in his hand.

"Too bad I am going to have to kill ya if you don't tell me somethin.'" Sam shoves the barrel into Eli's face, banging it against his nose, which causes him to stumble backwards.

Eli holds his face while blood flows like water from a faucet into his hands. "Okay! Okay! Shit!" Aggravated, Eli holds up one hand. "There was some . . . some sorta fight in the flatlands. A large man and some other man. I think I met the large man while I was on a run."

"A run? Where?"

Eli hesitates, trying to remember the area. "Uh, uh, shit. North side of Hock. Yeah, north."

"That doesn't help me!" Sam pulls the hammers back on the gun. He walks around Eli as if he is inspecting a slab of meat.

"Uh – uh. I don't know. I can't remember the name. A large group of run-down homes. An old neighborhood. All I can remember. Look – I just go and find what I need. I mind my business and keep moving."

"Old homes, huh?" Sam looks at Rahzy with one eyebrow raised. "Okay. Nice doing business with ya. Let's go, Rah!" Sam walks away.

As Rah walks pass, he knocks over some of the goods on Eli's display unit and looks back at him threateningly.

"Wait! What about my gun!" Eli shouts.

"You mean . . . *my* gun?"

Eli takes a moment to compose himself. He frowns as he watches the violent pair of strangers walk away with one of the finest goods he had in his possession. That he used to have in his possession. He quickly stands, wiping his nose and grabs just a few of his belongings. Without saying a word to his market neighbors, he embarrassingly runs away in the direction of his home.

"Eli! Where ya goin'?" Johnny shouts. "What about . . . your stuff?!"

The Creature Protruding

LANGSTON AND JESSE AWAKEN ON THE FRONT STEPS of the old man's home, after having finished off the last of the chips and bread which he provided. A small wheat loaf with walnut crumbs sprinkled on the top. A slightly unexpected, but appreciated gesture.

Jesse eliminates the dryness around his mouth while almost drinking all of the water. He hasn't had anything to fill his stomach since before he found Langston, with the exception of small snacks that he kept in his pocket.

"Hey, hey. Slow down, man. We need to save some." Langston reaches out toward Jesse. Jesse wipes his mouth as he hands him his bottle. Langston takes one last sip of his water before combining what was left into the two bottles. Then, he reapplies the top. He gains some composure before exhaling deeply, as he wonders about what is next.

"I guess we need to get to it."

"It looks like it's about to get dark again," Jesse replies after belching.

Langston nods before standing, walking down the path in front of the home. He assesses the area at the edge of the main road. His thoughts bounce from event to event; mental reflections on his travels up until now. Turn after turn; back and forth. *I'm tired,* he thinks.

"As long as we stay on one of these main roads," Langston pauses after sighing. "As long as we stay on these roads, we should be fine," he asserts.

Jesse tries to listen, but is consumed with having a full belly. He wipes breadcrumbs from his shirt as he stands, walking toward Langston. The two look at one another in a moment of silent reassurance before making their way to the nearby road, which ran parallel to the tall walls of Hock City. The road gradually split into multiple streets further out, like a tall tree with several branches; long and symbolic to Langston's journey.

This new part of their travels feels all too familiar. The roads, the view; the emotions stirring within Langston's being. He is confused, frustrated and anxious.

UHMANDRA

He feels like he has been pointed in every direction - a constant loop with no exit in sight.

The sound of the night dwindles as silence stretches across the desert land. Langston stops in his tracks, staring into the darkness. Jesse, unaware of Langston's sudden lack of movement, bumps into him.

"Why did you stop? What you doin'?" Jesse asks, looking around curiously.

"Need to take a leak."

Langston walks to the edge of the road where he turns his back. He starts to undo his pants just as the wind begins to stir. A crack of thunder startles him; echoing - before a spark, hidden behind dark clouds, lines the sky.

"Shit," Langston says.

"Mr. Langston?"

The wind becomes heavy as it gushes through the foliage; a type of wind of which Langston was all too acquainted.

"Run!" Langston screams.

"What--"

Before Jesse can ask his next question, Langston takes off down the road, running as fast as his endurance allows. Jesse wearily follows suit, but at a slower pace. "Why are we running?" he fearfully asks.

Jesse doesn't have as much experience as Langston in dealing with the desert flatlands in the dark, at least recently. And, darkness is coming. He had become a master of traversing the tunnels during his runs, using his ability whenever he could muster control of it. He avoided being outside the walls of Hock in the dark unless utterly necessary, especially with Madam Pearl constantly checking on his whereabouts.

Suddenly, the faint light from the sky darkens more. It fades enough where Langston can't see the ground in front of him. Thus, he veers from off the road and onto the desert sand. Moments later, the lightning flashes. It brings forth enough of a glow to show the landscape briefly.

"Ah, damn! Where is the road?! The road! We were supposed to stay on the road!"

"What — what should we do?" asked Jesse.

Langston continues to run, trying his best to inspect every inch of the area. He begins to see the same amber-colored eyes of which he was so fond: Desert

Dwellers. They are mostly behind him and Jesse, with enough distance between them to allow Langston to notice a large cave-like dwelling in front of him.

The dwelling appears to be protruding from the ground, resembling the mouth of a trapped creature who is trying to eat its way through the ground. Stoned, carved-like links are connected to the top and bottom of the dwelling, resembling teeth. On top of the dwelling are stacks of large square rocks, which have dark rectangular designs.

"Up there!" Jesse shouts, pointing.

"I don't think we gotta choice!"

The closer the two come to the rocks, the better they can see that they are approaching a city. A city built inside, around and atop of the large rock, was protruding from the ground. It was mostly hidden by thick fog which camouflaged it.

The fog seemed to grow thicker with each footstep, wrapping itself around Langston and Jesse like a large blanket.

"Man, I can't see!" screams Jesse.

"I got you! Stay close!"

Jesse grabs Langston's arm. An unnerving silence covers their path before they can take another step. Just as the silence appears, it leaves. It's followed by the faint sound of chanting in the distance. Then the sound of footsteps atop gravel follows. A voice yells out, speaking in the same foreign language with which Langston was all too familiar.

"Let's go!" Langston shouts again, not wasting time to investigate further.

"Stop!" A female voice emerges. "There is no need to fear us."

Langston continues to run, stumbling at times because of the poor level of visibility in front of him.

"Stop!" the voice shouts louder and more forcefully.

The ground quakes and the fog widens like a wall, causing Langston to stumble again. He crabwalks backwards, trying his best to move away from where he believes the person behind the voice is dwelling. Standing, he shoves Jesse to get behind him. They look ahead and notice the fog starts to clear, just enough to show a path leading toward the city within the rocks.

"Please, come to us," the voice speaks once more.

Langston and Jesse walk hesitantly through the mist-like fog. Desert Dwellers, standing at every corner of the cities' entrance, watch them closely while chanting something at a whisper.

"We won't harm you."

"Oh yeah? The last time I met your kind, you tried," Langston asserts, tensely.

"Our apologies for that. Please, come in."

"I rather not."

"Please. I will explain."

Langston stops purposely at the bottom of large stone steps. Jesse stands behind him as they both watch a tall person descend the steps, as if they were gliding. Once at the bottom, a slender woman - wrapped in layers of linen, removes her hood to expose her face. She has bronzed skin, with long, dark hair that is braided and hangs to her waist.

"My name is Kira and this is my home. These beautiful people are my family."

Langston looks around at the various faces near him. Faces that were similar to those he encountered early in his journey, in his attempts to get to Hock City - and once again, as he tries to make his way home.

"Desert Dwellers," Jesse adds, slightly trembling. His eyes grow wide.

"We have been called that, yes. But that is not who we are."

"Then who are you? And you speak --"

"Please, please. Come. I will tell you more inside, where it's safe."

At this moment, a thick fog reforms behind them near the city's entrance. The group of sand people - guarding the entrance - encloses Kira, Langston and Jesse inside of a circle. They walk deeper into the mouth of the rocks. The opening closes in such a way that it seems as if the rocks have swallowed them whole.

Nothin' Good Ahead

THE THICK, RICH ODOR OF DEATH AND REMAINS CIRCULATES THE SURROUNDINGS. Rancid air provided by the remnants of unpleasant leftovers drapes the area. The stench of the opposite of life; contrary to the living or anything good.

Kinth blinks his eyes slowly, and with each blink he notices something different. First, he notices the bleakness of the sky, peeking through a layer of heavy mist. He then realizes that he is lying on his back and is being transported somewhere. His hands and feet are bound as he lies inside a double layer of neuro-netting. He is strapped down to a large makeshift transport device.

He is annoyed by the squeak of the device's wheels, as well as the low sporadic thumps of the machinery. The contraption isn't used to transporting anything or anyone of this size. He exhales, as he looks up once more. The sky has a menacing smile, as if it has wicked plans for anyone brave enough to journey the area. The mist covers the landscape, as if it is tracking the travels of the group.

Kinth turns his head to his left and to his right. The sounds of footsteps are close, as well as the whisper of conversations. Light laughter and chuckles; the clearing of throats. He is certain that he is with one unit of The Guardian's men; destination unknown.

Wild, beastly dogs follow them. They growl, while exposing long, sharp teeth. They then circle, crisscrossing the rear and side areas of the group. They hope that their next meal arrives soon. Saliva hangs from their mouths, as anxiousness fills their eyes. Whining in excitement, they realize that regular meals are scarce.

Kinth notices the dogs and sighs. *May the flower of peace and light protect me,* he thinks. He locks eyes with one of the dogs, staring into the eyes of the apparent leader of the pack.

The more the group walks, the lower the land goes; darker in color – earthy and desolate. There are lumps of soil and rock; streaks of dark fluid resembling blood covers it all. The group reaches a steep decline, causing Kinth's body to slide around the transport device.

"Hey! Hey! You! You flunkies! Where y'all taking me?" he aggressively asks, looking around more. He struggles to sit up or to get a better view.

"Shut your trap!" a guard replies, jabbing him in the side with the blunt end of a spear. The spear releases a stream of electric volts which rapidly enter Kinth's body. It causes him to clench his teeth and groan from the pain. The blue hue of his veins brightens.

The group arrives at the edge of the road. What is left of an old light pole holds a mounted sign with a stenciled message: NO ENTRY. A large slab of rock holds another hand-drawn message: SERIOUSLY! NOTHIN' GOOD AHEAD!

Just beyond this pole is a rope, connected from one large stone on the left to one on the right side of the path. Beyond the rope, there is nothing more to be seen as the group approach a murky, open space.

"Let's go," the guard in charge says, unlatching one side of the rope.

The group walks through the opening, approaching a steep flow of steps. The steps wind downward, leading to a bridge which is long and extended. What is on the other side cannot be seen. From their vantage point, it appears as if it leads to nowhere. The columns of it descend into the depths below; beyond what the normal eye can see. The group can't see what is on the other side of the bridge or what is below it.

The wild dogs watch the group as they continue forward to an area where they have never traversed before. As much as they want to continue to keep the group's company, they turn away. They whine for new reasons as they leave, bowing out easily from following them any further.

Conversations end as the group wearily scans the handwritten message once more, as well as the eerie path ahead. The area is ominous and quiet – so quiet that some of The Guardian's most fearless men are hesitant to continue. They undecidedly look at one another, edging each other on without saying a word. No one wants to be the front man at this moment.

Kinth is removed from the cart, and bound to a large pole; carried like prey from a fresh kill. "You guys are in for some shit now. Seems like . . . there is something much more threatening around here than me," he says, sensing the apprehension of his captors. He is jabbed again, and passes out from the extra set of vigorous, electric volts that enters his body.

The unit carefully maneuvers down the steps, taking their time in order to move in sequence. Anything faster and they risk falling due to there are no nearby walls onto which to lean, not to mention enough ground to break their fall.

The clay steps somewhat crumble under the heaviness of the large entourage, with every stride made down the aged staircase. The unpleasant-looking staircase wasn't designed to welcome many visitors. At first look, it appears to have been designed to actually keep away trespassers.

The group nears the clearing, where the steps get closer to the bridge. Although, they first traverse several pillars. The pillars are aged - just as the stairs - and spaced apart just enough to deter wanderers. One missed step, and an unlucky person could plummet into the unknown.

One; two. One; two. The group takes turns moving in sequence - forward on the columns. Sweat practically pours from some of their brows as they reluctantly look down, only to adjust their footing and to locate the next column.

"Almost there, gentlemen. Nice and easy," the unit's captain whispers. "So far, so good," he adds quietly.

The group navigates another set of columns with ease before a gush of wind rushes them. The wind comes from above, forcefully shaking the columns, causing the men to become unstable. As the wind settles, the area becomes quieter than before. Suddenly something can be seen in the sky, moving around methodically in the distance.

"What is that?" a guard asks.

"GET DOWN!" Another from the group screams, after studying the movements of the object. A loud squawk blares from behind them, as the sound echoes from above.

Several of the guards try to run, hopping from column to column. One guard fumbles with his footing, almost falling. "MAN, FORGET THIS! THE GUARDIAN CAN KISS MY ASS!"

"NO, STAY TOGETHER! WE MUST STAY TOGETHER!" the captain yells before the thing in the sky shrieks again.

This time the squawk is louder, loud enough that it startles the guard who is trying to escape the area. He becomes distracted and misses a step, causing him to fall into the fog-covered depths.

His scream is loud and piercing at first, while then it fades to nothing at all. Nothing more than a nerve-wrecking silence.

"Oh man! Oh man! Oh man! Oh man!" Another from the group covers his ears to avoid hearing the screams.

"WHAT IS THAT?!" someone else asks, as he tries to keep his grasp on his part of the pole to which Kinth is bound to.

Kinth is still knocked out cold, unaware of how close he is to falling to a sudden death.

"C'MON! MOVE!" the leader of the group shouts again, continuing to navigate the path.

In the distance, the long creature flies in loops, circling the group from afar. It has reddish, scaly skin, smoky eyes and a spiked tongue. It cries again before stretching its wings wider, and flying further away. Then, it turns around and squints its eyes to gather information for its next attack.

"IT'S COMING BACK!"

"It's . . . it's trying to build momentum," another guard assesses.

"For what?"

The creature flies toward them, faster than before. It dives down just above them, grabbing a guard with its large mouth and razor-sharp teeth. It crushes the guard with one bite. Blood fills the air and splashes the group, covering them almost completely.

"SHIT!"

"LET'S MOVE!"

The group moves, ducking to avoid the terrifying attacks by the creature. They had moved enough where several of the men fall off of their beams. They fall like scattered dominos one by one. Other more fortunate guards were able to maintain their footing. They fight back, swinging large knives and machetes, while throwing spears to deter the creature. Some use their abilities to shield themselves from the attack, but nothing seems to keep the creature at bay long enough to escape.

Those not fighting have the task of holding onto Kinth. He is to be delivered to the planned destination by all costs. He is still unconscious, lying on his side across multiple columns. His head dangles over the column, while the pole to which he is attached slowly slides out of the men's hands. Between the size of Kinth and the size of the pole, keeping a grip on both was a task.

"WE GOIN' LOSE HIM!"

"NO! WE CAN'T! HOLD! HOLD HIM!" the leader responds.

At this point, there are only a few men left to muscle the task of transporting him. And they are faced with a decision: fight the winged-beast and risk Kinth falling or move as fast as they could toward the bridge while risking their own lives.

The creature dives again - grabbing another guard with so much force that it causes the entire group to fall from the columns. More screams ensue as the men fall at rapid speeds into the depths, reaching out with their hands as if they can be saved by the mist.

Kinth finally awakens, after feeling his stomach drop and the adrenaline rush through his body. The lapel and loose areas of his trench coat slap him in the face. At first he thinks he is dreaming, but as he looks around, he sees nothing but darkness from the depths and the small of the sky. He is certain that he isn't. He realizes that he is not floating in a natural bliss of a pleasant dream world. The sounds near him weren't natural. They were the screams of people, begging for another lease on life.

With a moment of strain, he breaks his wrist free from the pole, slowly undoing the straps around his ankles. He moves as fast as he can, despite being in a free fall. He then grabs the pole and with every morsel of power in his body, swinging it around like a sword and hoping to force it into something solid near him.

Nothing.

Well, ole boy. I guess this is it. Not how I imagined I would go out, he thinks. He releases the log, refusing to try to save himself any longer. He closes his eyes and relaxes his body, as he takes one last, deep breath.

Suddenly, the speed in which he travels decreases to a halt. Kinth opens one eye and then another, only to see the same fog-covered area around him. Everything around him seems suspended in the air. He then begins to float upward, just like some of the debris near him.

"What the hell?" he thinks aloud.

Slowly, he rises in midair, up from whence he came. He moves back toward the dim glow of the sky. He arrives above the columns, back near the bridge. He continues to float over the remaining beams above the bridge, through the mist toward a dwelling that is camouflaged by the fog around it.

He is the only one left because the rest of the group has met their demise. They have been devoured by the depths.

The closer Kinth comes toward the dwelling, the more he can see that it is made out of the same beams and stone which he had just crossed. It is a solid, castle-like structure with a wide, gate-covered opening. There is a gap in the path between the remaining part of the bridge and the gate. The gap is wide enough to deter most trespassers. Large windows with a deep green hue are on the front, and smaller windows with bars are on the sides.

Kinth is dropped onto the bridge, just before the gap. He lies on his back, noticing the creature that caused havoc just moments before is gliding in the air above him. While he is distracted, Kinth's wrists are bound quickly by several people who run away before they can be seen.

"Hey! What the – who are you?" Kinth shouts out.

A large creature - twice the size of Kinth or more - aggressively walks through the gate towards him. It resembles the creature in the sky, except that it was much smaller and without wings. And, it walked on two legs. It wears dark, industrial clothing and appears to have human-like mannerisms.

"Who are you?!" Kinth asserts himself again.

The creature grunts loudly, yanking him by his shackles. Kinth yanks back, preparing for another fight. The winged-beast in the sky shrieks, apparently co-signing its companion's actions from above.

A voice interrupts, "Don't strain yourself, sinner. Because I assure you . . . you won't win."

Scour the City

THE NOISINESS OF THE CITY RECEDES. A quiet falls over The Guardian's estate, after security activates the layer three security system. An extra set of walls rise from the ground, shielding the mansion from any danger lurking beyond Guardian's Grove. Security lighting embedded into the corner of each of these walls activates.

The mansion sits toward the back of the grove on a large section of hilly, tree-lined land just outside the main city. But, it's still connected to the pulse of the people inside the surrounding walls. Thick vines and fungus covers a portion of the vintage estate. Other small but similar homes are adjacent to the mansion, and mostly occupied by those on The Guardian's counsel.

The Guardian paces around his office, throwing back shots of ale he mixes with aged wine; wine which he brought up from the cellar. He inhales desert leaf that he has smoking inside a round, steel, and abstractly designed hotpot upon a portable countertop burner. The wine, in addition to the, desert leaf is a recipe for drunken order and misdirection. A toxic mix that creates hallucination, but he doesn't care.

He thinks aloud, visibly irritated. "As if I don't have enough bullshit to deal with . . . now this! Can't trust anyone. *ANYONE*."

The door to his office creaks.

The Guardian jolts his body around. "Where you been?!" he shouts, slamming the empty glassware on his desk. He pours more of the potent mixture before purposely falling backward into a plush, casual lounge chair nearby.

"I've been executing your orders. Did you miss me?" replies The Mantis proudly. He sits across from The Guardian in one of two adjacent chairs that have tall backs.

"Don't test me right now. It's not the time. Not . . . the time. You are supposed to be here!" One of The Guardian's legs shakes almost uncontrollably. He drinks again, leaning his head over the hotpot to enjoy another deep inhale. He raises his head while releasing smoke through his nose.

"How can I execute your orders if I am here with you?"

"That's not the point!"

"You are unraveling," The Mantis responds, undaunted.

The Guardian throws his glass against the wall, shattering it.

"You have a mess on your hands," The Mantis adds.

"I know this already! Shit!"

"So what did you plan to do about it?" asks The Mantis.

"Don't question me! Don't. . ." The Guardian jumps to his feet, mutating slightly. "I question you! You!" The color of his eyes flicker.

The Mantis remains unbothered and sits back silently.

"A human. A human! In my city! How is this possible! Huh? How? When I deliberately ordered their removal?!" The Guardian grabs a new glass, pouring himself another drink.

"Yes, you did. I know."

"So how is it possible?! I put you in charge of that!" The Guardian points at The Mantis emphatically.

"And I did what you ordered."

"Which was what? Refresh my memory. Pretend like . . . like I don't know anything," The Guardian replies sharply.

The Mantis sits back in his chair, clearing his throat. He makes assertive, slightly awkward eye contact before speaking. "We sectioned off every zone of the city, and one-by-one we quarantined every human we found. We escorted them away in quiet - as you instructed - with little if any disturbance; unlike now. This city is . . . well, anyway," he shakes his head and continues. "We worked with Mathias as you also insisted. We handed over all the humans we found to him in exchange for water and technology – anything he was willing to trade. It took many cycles, but we got it done."

The Guardian stares at The Mantis blankly, as if he understood little of what was being said. "Got it done," he chuckles softly.

"I haven't seen a human since. Well, that is until now," The Mantis continues.

The Guardian takes another sip before tilting his head back to stare at the ceiling. "What else? What did Mathias say he would do with the humans?"

"I didn't ask him anything more."

"Why not?" The Guardian sighs, frustrated.

"You did not instruct me to ask him what his plans for the humans would be," The Mantis states. "We used the technology and other supplies to get the water system installed. And the line system. The lights in and around the city, along with just about everything that relies on more than natural man power. The erection of the walls; the buildings. They were all built because of my efforts to do what you demanded; handing over bodies for the exchange of goods. You would remember this if you weren't —"

"Watch your tone in my presence," The Guardian snaps out of a hallucinogenic daze. "I know what the hell has been done. It's what hasn't been done that is in question."

"Are you implying that I haven't *done* something that you ordered?"

The Guardian doesn't respond immediately. Instead, he walks to his desk and sits in a chair behind it. "I don't make implications." He clasps his hands together, rubbing his thumbs together while thinking deeply. "Let's go have a talk with Mathias. Gather a unit for travel. Oh – and release my sister. I'm tired of seeing her face already. But keep an eye on her."

"But we just raised the security barriers."

"Well lower them!"

"Very well," The Mantis nods before exiting the room.

The Guardian turns his chair toward a large window and stares out into the horizon, seeing only the faint glow of the city coming from the opposite side of his estate. He then leans back in his chair, as he reaches into his pocket. He pulls out Langston's watch once again to study and admire it. Then, he closes his eyes as he falls into a deep sleep.

The Mantis makes his way down the hall toward the front of the mansion. Cluttered sounds of multiple footsteps grow loud behind him.

"Sir, sir! Something was in the room with Madam Pearl," guards excitedly approach.

"*Some-thing?*"

"Yeah. That rodent that normally hangs out at her casino. The one that helps run her place. He was in there."

"Where is he now?"

"We tried to get him, but he got away."

The Mantis scoffs. "And where is Pearl?"

"In the cellar."

"I will deal with her," The Mantis walks away.

The guards look at each other, puzzled by the lack of further information.

Madam Pearl paces around the cellar, multiple stories below the area where the conversation between The Mantis and the guards occurred. She drinks directly from one of the many bottles of wine, most of which is now destroyed due to recent events. She walks to the center of the room, where the large round table once in place lays in pieces on the floor. She examines the room in a concerned fashion, wondering what happened to cause this.

She also thinks about Kinth.

She notices folders and a pile of papers underneath one of the panels of wood. Focusing on the papers for a moment before grabbing one of the panels, she moves it aside for a better view. Underneath are various handwritten notes and photos of Pineville, Hock City and other places. Places with which she was unfamiliar.

UHMANDRA, one of the pieces of papers read at the top. She says the word aloud more than once, bewildered. On the back of the paper is a hand-drawn map of Hock City, as well as the other cities and corridors nearby. Longleaf, Fetela, Crown Lake. Some of the other names are smeared. Flipping through the rest of the papers, Pearl finds photos.

She studies the photos before hearing someone approach the cellar doors. The lock of the door is released before she can examine the photos and further inspect the documentation. She stuffs the documents into her waistband, concealing them underneath her blouse.

"Pearl," the Mantis speaks.

"Uh, uh – what you want?" Madam Pearl stammers. She fixes her clothing before the Mantis notices.

"Are you alright?"

Pearl nervously clears her throat. "You coming to do your master's dirty work, ain't ya? Hmm?"

The Mantis chuckles to himself. He walks slowly around the room, looking at what has become of the cellar, while examining the mess that was made.

"Nothing to say, servant boy?"

"Insulting me will do nothing but make your situation worse."

"Well, kill me and get over with, or whatever it is you came to do," Pearl kicks a piece of wood panel across the room.

"I don't want to harm you, Pearl."

"Then what do you want?"

"Nothing. Go back to your lascivious place of business and stay there."

Puzzled, Pearl stares at the Mantis.

"Go!" The Mantis startles her. "Nothing good will come of the changes here. Your sibling is not thinking with a level head right now. I suggest you stay inside. Go, before I change my mind."

Madam Pearl grows hesitant, frozen a bit in her movements before proceeding toward the cellar doors. She does her best to walk smoothly, keeping the papers inside her clothing from making noise. She turns around before exiting, saying, "I never wanted any of this." She waits for the Mantis to say something, but he doesn't.

"Get outta my way," Pearl continues, shoving one of her guards standing near the doors. "Can't believe you sided with my good-for-nothing brother. Let's go."

She climbs the stairwell to the main floor, forcefully exiting a side entrance. Then, she walks the bricked path around to the front of The Guardian's estate. While she does this, the Mantis makes his way to the front of the home, watching her departure from the front steps. As Pearl gets to the gates, armed guards look at Mantis for approval. He nods his head to the guards, as they open the security gates and allow her to pass through it.

Pearl brushes off her clothing of debris as she and her group of security walk through the gates expeditiously. Once far enough away from The Guardian's estate and away from the Mantis' view, she changes her course.

"Madam, the penthouse is this way," a confused guard states.

"I know where the hell MY penthouse is."

"So where are we going?"

"Somewhere else."

Transparency

LANGSTON AND JESSE CAREFULLY FOLLOW BEHIND KIRA.
The uncertainty the two feel within their souls can be seen
as they walk.

Kira and her entourage lead them deeper into the
large city which is carved from stone. Tall, wide columns
with intricate markings enclose various heavily guarded
entrances. Roped bridges connect the columns to various
individual dwellings. The fog is still thick at the borders,
engulfing the location like storm clouds. The environment
is quiet, as if most people are speaking in a whisper.

They travel through a set of obscure buildings and
various rooms before entering a large meeting hall. As
they walk deeper into the hall, their footsteps echo
against the walls. The rustling sound of their garments
travel through the open space like hums in the wind.

A roundtable sits in the middle of the hall upon a platform, elevated by several stairs. The table has similar markings as the columns, engraved mostly in the center, along with several chairs positioned around it.

"Please, join me," Kira extends her hand toward the table.

Langston and Jesse cautiously climb the steps, taking a seat at the table. Kira sits directly across from them. Desert Dwellers fill every other seat, as well as stand around the room. They are all draped in some sort of brown or tan garment; linen or cargo attire, repurposed potato sack clothing and more. Every eye is on the visitors.

"You – you Desert Dwellers. Y'all don't look the same like out there. When I saw you – on my way to Hock . . ." Langston bolts into the conversation. "And you - you talk normal. I can understand you. Your words were different before."

"Please," Kira places her hand on the table, "I respectfully ask that you address us by our actual name. We are the Ekladi people. Most don't know who we are; so instead, they fear us, and they label us. They have created their own terms to describe us. And yes, we do speak like you. But we also have our own method of communicating with each other."

"Your own language?" Jesse asks.

Kira smiles gently. "Something like that. My people have been around for quite some time. Some of us were once members of the society living behind those walls. But as you can see, we are no longer within or welcomed inside of those walls. To survive and for privacy, we created our own way of sending messages to each other."

"But what *are* you? I saw some of you, like, like – die and come back to life," Langston replies.

"We are like you," Kira replies before turning her head to look at Jesse, "and you. And many of the others out there."

"You're human?" Langston asks, mildly excited.

"Well, see – there is no simple answer to that."

"What you mean?"

"Technically, we are all human or come from humans. Since the historical event - where the atmosphere changed. Humans most knew before were changed. Those who were born thereafter are not completely human. They are unique like you, Jesse." Kira lightly places her hand on the table.

"How did you know?" Jesse asks.

Kira smiles again before turning toward a young woman near, to who she nods. The woman then stands, closing her eyes for a moment. The color of her entire body begins to change: her skin, hair, eyes and clothing. She blends in with the table completely, changing her color to blend in with the chair in which she had been sitting.

Jesse is stunned.

"A person of 100% human genetics has not been seen in quite some time. Like you, Jesse, many of us have something special about us. Some amongst us can change their appearance to camouflage themselves. I believe you can do the same. Can you show us?"

Langston turns his attention to Jesse, at times looking at the young woman as well. Jesse sits back in his chair and looks down, unsure on what to do.

"Jesse, it's okay. You are safe amongst me and my people."

"But y'all attacked me," Langston interjects.

"My apologies for that. We operate like most in the wild. We only attack when we feel threatened. Most people don't wander when it's dark. You unknowingly crossed our path, and we reacted."

"But how did y'all come back like that? I saw Kinth shoot and kill some of your people. And he talked just like you. It was like he understood you."

"Your associate has lived amongst us for quite some time. That abandon business he dwells in sits right in a territory we frequent. He has learned some of our ways and words, it seems." Kira then turns toward a large, muscular man standing a few feet away. She nods at him. The man takes a few steps closer to the table and lowers his head. His body begins to blur. Suddenly a copy of himself extracts and stands beside him.

"Wow, it's like – like a mirror!" Jesse exudes.

"Yes. Any movement by the source controls the copy," Kira adds.

Kira nods one last time and others from the Ekladi people approach. Each one displays something unique about themselves, such as their ability to change their appearance and control objects with their minds. Some of the others have no abilities but their physical features are modified.

"Only a few of us have abilities. We use these skills you see before you to survive. Collectively, this works.

Sometimes we purposely manipulate our surroundings to give off a larger, more dangerous appearance than what we really are. When you met my people, we were out looking for resources and food."

"What do you mean, 'manipulate'?" Langston asks.

"In the wild, some animals enlarge themselves or make aggressive sounds to fend off predators. We do this as well. We make unusual noises and move erratically, as well as leave carcasses from our food - to give the appearance we are a deadly species. When in reality, we are just trying to survive like everyone else. We aren't the real threat out here."

"Then who is?"

"If you travel the wrong path, you will likely find out whom," an anonymous Ekladi elder speaks from the other end of the table.

"You mean there are more threats than the people I just dealt with behind those walls?"

Kira nods.

"Damn . . . and this historical event that you speak of . . . what happened exactly? I have only heard bits and pieces about it. Until I came here, I only knew where I lived. Didn't realize there was more out here. Like the other corridors," Langston inquires.

"Oh, yes! Much, much more! Corridors, cities, sections - kingdoms. These words all mean the same. And honestly, bits and pieces of knowledge about the origin of these areas is all that most have. Because the event you speak of happened so long ago. But I can share what I know.

"At one point, the seven cities - or corridors as you said - were connected. It was one large piece of land with many different people living collectively. It was a beautiful environment. The grounds were lush and green; the water was clear and flowing. The mountains stretched from every end of the sky." Kira's eyes light up, almost like the glow of the neon signs in the city. She smiles as she speaks, proud of the times she remembers and was told about.

"Then what happened?" Langston is fixated on the story.

"Suddenly a great storm came. The storm divided the land, and our world became dark. People and families were torn apart, becoming lost in the darkness for many, many days."

"Dark how?"

"Every day - all day - was night. Some days were darker than others. The people couldn't see their feet in front of them. They tried their best to continue with normal lives, but not much could be done with the dark around them."

"So what did they do?" Jesse asks.

"At some point, they couldn't keep up with what day it was. So they began to count the cycle pattern of when the light came and when the light left. They used anything they could to help them keep up with the patterns, but after a while, the task became too much to track. So, they trusted their instincts as best that they could. In between this effort, they were resourceful. They worked together to survive at first."

"At first?" Langston leans in and rests his arms on the table.

"Yes. They did what they could until people started to change slowly. The storm in the atmosphere did something to them. They changed, both mentally and some physically. As time passed, they noticed these changes about themselves. Some used their changes for good. Others didn't. What you see out there is the combined result of this."

Langston looks down at his hands and then over at Jesse.

"You are traveling somewhere? Yes?" Kira asks.

"Trying to get home."

"Where is home?"

"Longleaf."

"I have never been that way, but some of my people know which direction you will have to travel to get there. I can spare some of them to lead you to the border. They can protect you. Once at the border, you will have to move forward on your own."

"What border?" Jesse asks. "Y'all don't travel underground or use the doorways?"

"You're referring to the tunnels?"

Jesse nods as he begins to fiddle with the key around his neck.

"Is that a key to one of the doorways?" Kira inquires again.

"Yeah. To Hock."

"Does that key work for any other doors?"

"I – I never tried other doors."

"I see. But to answer your question, no. Those doorways are dangerous, and those tunnels are limited. They only extend right around the Pines and to some evil places. Only those that need to hide and are afraid to travel in plain sight use those. Hock is not a place of transparency and purity, so this is why most from there travel this way. The borders are where all the lands used to connect."

"The bridges," Langston presumes.

"Yes. Most of the bridges are dwindling. Soon, there will be no way to reach the various lands."

"But . . . what about the doorways I saw?"

"The doorways are guarded by the gatekeepers, but most of them lead to darker places. Most that live and move underground don't want to be seen. Most that don't want to be seen have something hide. My people do not have anything to hide. We only hide for survival."

"Well . . . let's go." Jesse stands to his feet and brushes off his pants. "What's up with the fog?" He points out.

Langston looks around, noticing that the fog begins to border the room.

"It's more of a mist than fog. Some of us can control natural elements like the condensation in the air. We use this to our advantage -"

"To hide," Langston says.

"Yes."

"Man. That's pretty cool," Langston rubs his chin. "Okay. Like the kid said, we need to get going. Thanks for clearing things up. And I appreciate you helping us."

Kira turns toward a group of Ekladi citizens, nodding once more. They turn with precision as they head toward the room's exit.

"It is my pleasure. My people will guide you to the border, but no further."

"How long will this take?" Langston asks.

"Time is of no matter for something this important."

Langston silently agrees.

"But you will get there," Kira adds, softly. "You will get there."

A Little Recon

WITH EACH STEP THAT RAHZY AND SAM MAKE TOWARDS the outskirts of the city, the sounds of uproar and mayhem fades. They silently traverse the main roads of the Pineville flatlands, keeping their eyes open for any clues which might lead them to the human previously seen in Hock.

Rahzy glides through the air, circling the area widely before landing near Sam. He looks at his counterpart hard before sighing; various thoughts floating around in his mind. He senses that Sam is planning ahead by the way he is focused on the ground in front of him.

"You think he was telling the truth?"

"Who?" Sam inquires.

"That guy. Mr. Ballsy, back at that market," replies Rahzy.

Sam chuckles. "Doesn't really matter. This direction takes us back to base. We don't have to stray far to find that old neighborhood. Shit. I think we passed it on the way in, but we were inside the walls. So, we couldn't see it. And we gotta nice weapon out of the deal." Sam admires the gun that he took from Eli at the Exchange.

The two are again briefly silent.

"Besides, I could see the fear in his eyes. Probably got somethin' to lose. A family. Didn't want to risk their safety. Don't think he wasn't lying," Sam shakes his head, continuing.

"I guess we will find out." Rahzy reaches out toward Sam. "Let me see that."

Sam hands him the gun, to which Rahzy smells it deeply. "I'm going to expand out. Do some recon. See what I can find. I'll meet you," he says, giving the gun back to Sam.

"Just meet me somewhere right before North Hock, and don't start anything without me. Okay, Buttercup?" Sam says.

Rahzy waves off Sam's cheeky comment before zooming away in the adjacent direction. He flies out several miles and circles the area, only to be greeted by more desert flatland. He further sees the remains of homes and businesses. Not a person in sight. He lands upon a stack of smashed cars stored in a field near Highway 99.

A vague, but familiar scent is close which leads him toward the station in which Kinth dwelled. He draws his weapon as he gets closer, moving into the area carefully. The place is quiet except for nearby rodents and birds, along with the sound of loose gutters. It becomes even more silent as the sky starts to darken.

He enters through the backdoor to avoid possible traps, and to perhaps surprise whoever may be inside. The door creaks as he tiptoes inside. The air smells familiar as he inspects the surroundings, noticing a door to an office. He follows the scent into the office, which matches the scent of the gun.

Entering the office, he gently picks up various papers and utensils, smelling each. He sits in the chair behind the desk and closes his eyes. Through his slight retro cognitive abilities, he can feel the presence of someone who was once sitting where he sat, while doing similar actions. But he can't get a clear picture of the person; just the shape and blurred visual of the scene.

He absorbs the information from the office before gradually journeying down the hall, passing a wall with various photos. He enters a room that has two cots and a wooden nightstand. Fumbling through the cots and the nightstand, he eventually finds a thin scrapbook. And so, he flips through the pages quickly before heading toward the station's lobby.

The scent of the station thus far has been heavy and solitary at times but begins to blend with another as he walks more into the station's lobby. The new, unusual odor is one that he hadn't come across before.

Glass is on the lobby's floor, and based on how sparse it is in certain areas, Rahzy can tell that it has been recently walked upon. He kneels down to inspect it closer, at which point he notices a small spec of blood nearby. He retrieves a sample of it before heading outside to the front of the station. The glow of Hock City is in the distance, at the end of a long stretch of road which also stretches to the other direction. Layers of mountainous hills are also in the distance.

With little effort, Rahzy then jumps into the air and spreads his wings. He zooms in a modified direction from whence he came; toward the northern territory of the Pines, near Hock.

The view from above is both daunting and astounding, like the view at dusk, resembles ocean water at night. There is little light except for the glow of the city. The tall hills are intimidating and connect to larger mountains; mountains which surround the remains of residential neighborhoods.

Rahzy glides steadily before noticing someone kneeling behind a partially condemned wall, not far from a neighborhood's entrance. *Could this be the place?* he thinks. Yards away, a small number of people walk in a tight knit group within the neighborhood.

Rahzy circles the area, as high and as quietly as possible thereby avoiding being seen for what he is. Not the same old desert bird looking for scraps, but a half-man-half Ferruginous assassin with other abilities.

He lands aside Sam, who had apparently been following the group for a while.

"So?" Sam asks.

"Nothing but this." He hands Sam the scrapbook. "Found a place that had a similar scent as that old man's house. And found some blood."

Sam looks at the scrapbook, mouthing the information as he reads. "Human blood?"

"Could be. The human has been in this area, definitely."

"What is this?"

"I don't know. Looks like some sort of . . . family album or something."

Sam continues to study.

Rahzy looks ahead. "Who is that?" he whispers.

"Dunno. I heard them a ways back. Been following them since. They almost noticed me. By the looks of how they're moving, they're up to something. Or, headed somewhere important."

"Is that a chick in the middle?"

"From what I can tell," Sam scratches his head. "Looks like they are protecting her."

"Do they have abilities?"

"Dunno."

Nearby, Madam Pearl and her small group of security walk towards her uncle's estate, not knowing they are being followed. Not much is said between the members of her team. Only the sounds of footsteps, heavy breathing and coughing - due to the movement of the desert wind - ensue.

"That's far enough," Madam Pearl shouts an order. She stops and looks ahead while catching her breath.

"Are you sure, Madam?"

"Yeah. Y'all can't go no further. Wait here."

The group positions themselves at various points on the road between the homes. Madam Pearl continues on by herself, at times gazing over her shoulder and rubbing her arms. It's getting chilly and it has been many cycles since she has seen her uncle. Nervousness covers the inner layer of her hard exterior.

Pearl has been away for a good while, and so her guards grow restless. They pace around the area and are not keeping a watch as they are supposed to do. They are preoccupied with one-on-one conversations amongst other shenanigans.

"Man, I'm really tired of all this." One guard speaks to no one in particular, after double-checking that Pearl was far enough away.

"What's that?" another guard asks.

"This. What we have been doin'."

"Yeah; I feel ya.'"

"We get yanked back and forth to do all their dirty work, and for what? Just to be able to live inside that place?"

"Yeah."

"Shit. It's not much better than out here."

"Bullshit. Can't find food and girls out here like we have in there."

"You and these girls. Is that all you think about?"

Another guard arms his weapon and approaches the group. "Man, y'all better shut the hell up before she hears you. Between her and The Guardian, they can both help you retire from your role . . . with no problem. You follow my orders, which are *her* orders. If you want out, you know the way out."

The complaining guards quiet their words quickly, clearing their throats as they spread out.

Sam listens to the guard's conversations while he follows Pearl in a parallel field. He watches her closely as Rahzy studies the area from above. After a few moments of this, Rahzy then lands near Sam again.

"Pearl . . . who is this Pearl?" Sam thinks aloud.

"What's the move?" Rahzy asks.

"Take 'em out. Then we get closer to Ms. Thing here. There is something different about this group."

"Kill 'em?"

"No. That will draw unnecessary attention."

Without saying a word, Rahzy takes off into an alternate direction. He flies far enough away to avoid being seen by the group of guards below. Once he's high into the sky, he loops around a few times to build up the air beneath him. With the momentum he creates, he flies down toward the group of distracted guards and pounces on some of them in one motion. Before the other untouched guards can respond, he bolts towards them. He disarms them, knocking them unconscious.

Madam Pearl hears some of the commotion from where she is, but waves it off as she approaches the walkway to her uncle's home. *Idiots,* she thinks. Her stomach tightens the more she thinks about all that has happened. As she gets closer to the door, she is greeted by a voice she hasn't heard in a long while.

"What do you want, child?" the voice speaks.

"I need to see you."

"But you aren't alone."

"Just a few of my men; watching out for me. Please, let me in."

"Hurry inside," the voice scoffs.

The door to the home opens slowly. Madam Pearl shuffles into the entrance quickly. She walks down the hall to the library.

"You are not alone."

"Uncle?" She doesn't see him yet.

"Who are these people you have brought with you?"

"Huh? I didn't bring anyone with me other than my security."

"Well, it seems someone other than your security is here."

"Who?"

"There is another presence here. You have made my home vulnerable, so make this quick."

Madam Pearl, confused, jogs to a window and looks out into the road. She stares hard out of the window, but because of the distance and the darkness, she can't see that her group of guards has been attacked. She turns around and scratches her head.

"It's a mess in the city."

"You came all this way to remind me of this?"

"No, uncle. A real mess. Kinth came back . . . and him and Franklin got into it. I don't know where he is now. I think Franklin did somethin' to him and to Daddy. I don't know what the hell goin' on. And now - now I fear that Franklin will do anything to control everything. I don't know where Jesse is. That damn human done caused an uproar."

"Why all of a sudden do you care? Haven't you been doing whatever he says? Why now? Hmm?"

Pearl gazes at the floor.

Her elder uncle reveals himself from behind one of the bookshelves in the room. He walks over to his desk and sits in the chair behind it, looking over Pearl.

"Goodness, child. What has happened to you?" Uncle inquires.

"What's happened to me? What's happened to you? You – you aged."

"Yes, yes. I know. But it doesn't seem like life has treated you well in that city."

"Doesn't seem like that city has done either one of us any good," Pearl replies.

Uncle chuckles.

"I guess that's why I am here." Madam Pearl responds, slightly offended. "I also found these. What is goin' on? Do you know anything?"

Pearl reaches inside her clothing, pulling out the papers she had hidden. She tosses them onto her uncle's desk.

Uncle takes a look at the papers. He clears his throat a few times before grabbing a pencil and paper. Pearl watches on as he begins to write, perturbed. He shows what he has written with each complete thought he manages to jot down.

SOMEONE IS LISTENING OUTDOORS. SO DON'T SAY ANYTHING FROM THIS POINT FORWARD. NOT A WORD. JUST LISTEN.

Madam Pearl is startled by the news, but nods.

TWO PEOPLE HAVE BEEN FOLLOWING YOU FOR A SHORT TIME. I DON'T KNOW IF THEY ARE FROM THE CITY. THEY ARE LOOKING FOR SOMEONE AND BELIEVE YOU KNOW WHERE THAT SOMEONE IS. I SUSPECT THEY ARE LOOKING FOR THE HUMAN.

THE HUMAN CAME HERE WITH YOUR RUNNER. HE IS TRYING TO FIND HIS PLACE OF ORIGIN.

"What about Kinth? And Daddy? And these papers?" Madam Pearl forgetfully asks aloud.

Uncle puts his index finger over his mouth, tapping his lips before writing more.

KINTH IS FINE, FOR THE MOMENT. BUT THE FURTHER AWAY HE GOES, THE LESS I CAN SEE OF HIM. I HAVE NOT SEEN YOUR FATHER IN AGES. I HAVE NO UPDATE ON HIM. ALL I CAN SAY ABOUT THESE DOCUMENTS IS - THEY ARE THE REASON YOUR FATHER HAS GONE MISSING.

Outside, Sam and Rahzy approach the home quietly. They crouch down, strolling around the home until they can get a better listen of the conversation inside. They position themselves where they can hear the last few words spoken between Madam Pearl and her uncle, but then the conversation falls to a hush.

"Let's go in," Sam says, cautiously.

Sam punches a hole through a side glass door, causing a loud thrash throughout the home. He reaches inside the opening he creates and unlocks the door. The noise alarms both Madam Pearl and her uncle.

"Go! Quickly! Out the backdoor," Uncle says. "Get away from here, child! But please - not back to that city! I will try to disguise you as much as I can."

"But what about these papers?"

"There is no time! Go!" Uncle grabs the papers and quickly stuffs them away.

As Pearl tiptoes toward her only exit, her uncle stands perfectly still and closes his eyes. His home is full of doors upon reopening his eyes. Every normal wall is converted into some type of door, some with more than one handle and lock. He sits on a pile of books and closes his eyes again.

"What the . . ." Sam and Rahzy are trapped inside of a loop of doors. Rahzy grabs the nearest door handle and turns it. It opens but leads to a room with even more doors.

"Okay, wise guy! You can either come out and answer a couple questions, or we will destroy this place till we get to you! Every door! I mean it!" Sam yells. He plows through one of the doors with his fist, shattering it.

"I don't know who you are, but there is nothing for you here!" Uncle shouts from his library.

"Ah, don't be like that! We just want to know where he is! And then we will go! Okay?! Simple!"

"I have no idea who you are referring to!"

"Yeah you do! The human! Where is he? And where is the woman?"

While Sam launches questions, Rahzy closes his eyes. He concentrates deeply, as he begins to see the vague silhouette of a person in an adjacent room. He turns his body around and can sense that other people had visited the elderly man as well.

"He is in there," he whispers to Sam.

"The human?"

"No, but the human has been here, too."

"Okay! You got one last chance to share what you know! Or, we are coming in there!"

"Do what you must!" Uncle prepares himself.

Sam grows even more frustrated as he and Rahzy pound against the doors leading to the library where Uncle awaits. The elderly uncle creates another layer of barriers with every door smashed in, hoping to stall the intruders as long as possible. He keeps this effort going for as long as he can before his strength begins to dwindle. He walks over and falls back into his chair, breathing heavily.

Rahzy then bursts through one of the barriers and positions himself behind him. He grabs the elderly man by the neck and shoulders, lifting him into the air. Sam follows through the opening as he stands in front of the weary, old man.

"Make this easy on yourself, sir. I'm not a fan of hurting old people, but I will if I have to," Sam says.

"We know the human has been here. I can smell him! Where is the girl? She knows where he is, doesn't she?!" Rahzy chimes in.

"Okay, okay!" The old man struggles, unable to fight against the strength of the grasp. "What has happened to the good in you people?!"

"Put him down." Sam gives the old man a moment to collect himself. He sits in a chair and stares at him, while Rahzy maintains his position. "So – where is he?"

"I will tell you if you promise not to hurt me or the woman who left here."

"I might be able to do that."

"Ah, what does it matter? You don't seem like someone who keeps their word anyway." Uncle waves his hand, coughing.

Sammy shrugs.

"He's at Del –"the old man strains to speak, feeling faint. "Delrusia Island."

Sam turns toward Rahzy, "You heard of this place?"

Rahzy shakes his head.

"Are you bullshittin' me, old man?"

"No. I'm not. The human is headed there to find his brother. The island is on the other side of the city."

"Then why did that chick come out here layered up with all the heavy hitters?"

"She was just making a delivery to me. She checks on me from time to time. I always request that she doesn't travel alone."

Sam skeptically stands to his feet as he maintains eye contact with the elderly man. He looks over at Rahzy who has a similar expression.

"Okay, old man. Just remember that we know where you live now."

"Turn this place back to normal so we can get outta here," Rahzy says before walking over to Sam. "We're just going to believe what he says?"

"Look at him. He ain't goin' nowhere. If he's lyin,' we just come back and kill 'em."

"What about the entourage we saw on the way in?"

"How about we catch up to 'em, and say hello?" Sam whispers.

Just yards ahead, Madam Pearl stumbles, losing her footing as she presses her way through the open field. She fights through tall grass and long stems from dried brush, which slaps her across her torsos as she moves quickly toward Hock City.

She cringes after she hears the slight screams of her uncle, unsure on what is happening to him. Seeing her guards, Pearl realizes that they're lying around just steps away. Beaten and battered.

"Get up, you fools!"

The team is slow to rise, holding their heads and extremities in pain.

"We gotta go!"

Delrusia Island

THE STENCH OF MADNESS AND DECAY swarms every inch of the suspicious, unfamiliar area - like a flock of birds feeding on animal remains, or a pack of wolves gathering to tear the meat of their prey from its bones.

The cold, empty smell of desertedness seeps into Kinth's being with each step he takes into the environment. He studies the halls of what appears to be a makeshift prison, carved from stone and embedded with iron. The leftover parts from a bridge effort abandoned, which is somehow suspended away from nearby land.

The prison is positioned in a fashion where visitors are advised by its visual appearance to stay away, but once they pass a certain point, there is no use in trying to turn around.

Kinth is still being pulled by the creature that is much taller and larger than he is. The creature has lumps of blackened, torched skin atop massive, mutated muscles. There are deep scars randomly placed across its body. Kinth wonders what caused the wounds.

The creature says nothing, speaking with only its eyes and facial expressions, while grunting sporadically. It throws Kinth into a circular cell; one that is large enough for the usual, average-sized captives but barely large enough for the new captive's stature. Handprints, scratches and the dried residues of fluids fill almost every inch of the cell walls.

"Hey! What the fuck is this place?! What am I doin' here?" Kinth shouts through the bars after the abstractly-designed gate is slammed shut in front of him. He grabs at the bars, trying to bend and move them but is struck on his hands by the, seemingly, always irritated creature standing nearby.

"He has become quite good at that," someone says.

Kinth recognizes the voice as the same one he heard outside the gates. "Why the hell am I here? Why didn't you let me die?" he responds.

UHMANDRA

The dragging sound of footsteps gets louder. A shadow begins to show against an adjacent wall before a tall, slender man appears. He is wearing a dark colored bucket hat, oddly designed clerical collar and overcoat. The clerical collar is made of copper with engraved jagged lines.

The man doesn't say anything as he watches Kinth from behind a pair of thick sunglasses, with a bit of a smirk on his face. His fists appear to be clinched in his pockets, juggling something around in one hand.

"Why the hell am I here?!" Kinth asks again. "What is this place?"

The slender man takes turns, leaning on his toes and his heels. "You, sinner, are on Delrusia Island!" He screams the name loud, causing other inmates to grow excited. They bang on the bars of their cells violently.

"Where?"

"Here is where you will spend the rest of your life as you know it, repenting your sins."

Kinth's frown deepens. "What you talkin' 'bout?"

"Confess of your sins, sinner."

"What? What are you? Some sorta priest?"

The man paces up and down the narrow, cobble path in front of Kinth's cell. Nearby, there are other cells filled with various types of people and creatures. Most are preoccupied with their own activities, including the voices and conversations in their heads. Some listen to the exchange between the slender man – of who they are all too fond - and the new arrival.

"Sinner! Confess!"

Kinth watches the man closely, but doesn't respond.

The slender man clears his throat before extending one of his hands outwards above him. "This place is where sinners come to repent for their bad deeds for the rest of their lives if need be, and in darkness, nonetheless. The killings; the lies; the hate. The stealing; looting. The constant take, take, take. SINS! So, get comfy, sinner. This is home now."

"SINNER!" a random captive screams, co-signing what the slim man said.

"Bullshit! Man, you better let me outta here!" Kinth bangs against the bars as distress covers his face.

The large creature roars and flexes its muscles in response to Kinth's tone and body language.

UHMANDRA

"Silence, sinner! You will address me by 'Sir Grace'! Because it is I and only I who can provide you with grace and mercy within this place." The slim man turns his back and walks toward another cell. "You will answer my question soon enough. Until you do, your time won't begin," he says, before laughing and walking away.

The creature follows behind the slim man at a much more sluggish pace. It bangs its hand against the various cell bars and doors, forcing the detainees to quiet down.

Kinth shakes his head before resting against the back wall of the cell. He looks up and around, trying to figure out where he is and how to escape. There are only walls and bars and the sounds of nothingness now around him. *Awfully quiet for a prison,* he thinks.

He stands again, looking out the small opening on the back wall made of the same gated material which held him inside the cell. He could vaguely see the winged creature in the distance, looping around throughout the dreary area, as quietly as its size will allow.

Kinth grunts as he pulls at the bars of the window, trying once more to free himself.

"Don't waste your time, man."

Kinth approaches the front of his cell, hopefully getting a look at the new person behind the voice. He can't see the person, who is apparently in the cell bedside his. He looks down, and tries to calm the shake in his hands.

"Those bars – they put something on 'em. They're different. Even the strongest in here can't break 'em. Trust me," the voice continues.

"Put something on 'em? Like what?"

"Dunno. But you're wasting your energy."

Kinth sighs before turning around and sitting down closer to the shared wall near the front of the cell.

"What you in for?"

Kinth doesn't reply. The first thing he thinks is that this person could be working for the man running this place. So instead, Kinth strokes his beard, while breathing slowly but heavily. His belly aches. He has been so focused on the recent events that he has denied himself food, only to replace it with dirty water and ale as well as the few nuts leftover in his pockets.

"Ah. One of those. The quiet type. A man with secrets. All good. We all got those. We all come in here the same way. But to get thrown in here, you must've done something serious."

Kinth sighs deeply. "Doesn't matter what I done."

"Man! You sound familiar. You sure I don't know you? You from Hock?" The voice gets louder. From the sound, the man has quickly moved closer to the shared wall.

"Doesn't matter."

"The only thing that doesn't matter, is matter — 'cause matter is everywhere."

"What?"

"Nothing." The person chuckles. "Just a lil' something I heard before. What's your name at least? Everybody needs a friend."

The wind stirs outside the barred windows, drawing Kinth's attention. For a moment, he oddly feels like he's back at the station.

"SINNER!" The random prisoner across the way yells again, breaking Kinth's concentration.

"I don't have a name," Kinth finally replies.

"What?! A man with no name?! Noooo! Not possible."

Kinth raises an eyebrow because the person's voice is becoming familiar to him, too. He then closes his eyes, resting his head on the wall while struggling to make sense of where he was and why he was there. If he had left that human alone, where would he be? He knows that his brother is one of the reasons he has been sent to this place, but what are the other reasons? "Names aren't important anymore," he replies.

"What does a man have if he doesn't have a name?"

"He has his actions. Sometimes you don't need anything but action. Words . . . don't have much weight anymore."

"Ah! I like that! I like that! A man of action is a man of reverence."

An eerie clink sound subtly rings throughout the cluster of cells. The sound of a bell, struck gently but hard enough to echo.

"SHHH!" A random prisoner across from the conversation rapidly claps his hands. He then extends one of his scaly hands through the bars and points.

"What's goin' on?"

"Oh, it's chow time. That crazy dude over there clappin' doesn't have a name. So I call him Mr. Shush. He always shushin' us before the food comes. His favorite part of the day, I guess. The dude screamin' down there doesn't have a name either. I didn't bother to give him one yet. I'm Aldo. I-"

"Aldo?" Kinth's eyes widened as he stands to his feet. He approaches the gate of his cell quickly. "Aldo? From Hock?"

"Kinth? Oh shit! I knew I recognized that voice." Aldo extends his hand as far as he can through the bars of his cell toward Kinth.

"Shh, don't say my name," Kinth does his best to shake Aldo's hand, but can only grip a portion of his fingers.

"Man, if you in here, they already know your name."

"SHHH!" Mr. Shush interjects.

Another similar, but smaller creature walks the path between the cells, throwing medium-sized sacks into each. Mr. Shush catches his sack and bolts to a corner of his cell.

"Please don't throw mine. The last time you threw it too hard and smashed it all up, jerk," Aldo says.

The creature squints its eyes, grunting before throwing the bag anyway. They throw it hard enough that the sack hits Aldo in the chest, knocking him to the floor. It then walks pass Kinth's cell without stopping, and grunts again.

"Hey, prick! Where is mine?!" Kinth yells.

"You gotta give 'em somethin,'" Aldo says.

"Huh?"

"You won't eat until you *repent,* whatever the hell that means. Just tell 'em anything. If you don't, they will move you."

"Move me where?"

"Dunno. Clearly I told them something since I am still right here with my sack. All I know is the last dude in here was like you. Older dude; never saw or heard him 'cause he refused to speak. He was in a cell somewhere down there. But they moved him. Haven't heard about him since."

"I'll take my chances."

"Still proud, I see," Aldo chuckles. "Gotta eat something, man. Only thing that keeps you sane down here. The conversation and the food, no matter how bad they both are."

"They got any ale?"

"That's all they got! No water down here. Or none that you want, at least. But it ain't good, though."

"How did you end up in here? I didn't know this place existed. We've been to a lot of areas around the seven lands, and I have never heard of this place." Kinth lays down and rests his head on the palms of his hands, staring at the roof of his cell.

Aldo does his best to chew chunks of hot potatoes before responding. "Man! I thought you were dead. When your brother took over, he gave his men free reign to do whatever they wanted. His men killed most of our team . . . for *any* reason! Killed anyone who still backed your father's leadership. I thought they got you, too."

"No. But some days I wish they had."

Aldo scoffs, "Fortunately for some of us —like me, who surrendered— we were spared."

"Spared?"

"Yeah, man. Most of your father's counsel was forced out the city. Including the security folks – like us – who protected him. We were separated, and some of us brought here."

"You were threats," Kinth speaks, now while gazing through the bars of his cell.

"Exactly. Put us all together and we are a force. Separate us and not so much."

"Yeah."

"But I'm sorry about your Pops. Do you know where he is? Is he alive?"

"Don't know."

"Hope so. He was a good man. Fair. Where you been all this time?" Aldo asks, slightly exasperated. His chewing slows down.

"He was. He was." Kinth sighs. "I've been in the Pines laying low. Before the mess my brother made, Father ordered me to do recon."

"Recon for what?"

"He wouldn't tell me much. Just that he had a project. He had to assess available land throughout the

Pines, between Hock and the other corridors. I wasn't supposed to be gone long, but the mission took longer than expected. On my way back, I saw many familiar faces leaving the city. Most of them told me that something had happened. But no one knew what. They were . . . just worn out. Battered people. I . . . I tried to get back, but one of the people had a message for me."

"A message?"

"Yeah. A message from Father. He told me not to return. He didn't tell me why or explained much. He – he just told me not to come back. Then I heard about the changes; the craziness. I wanted to come back, but it would have been suicide. I grew angry, so angry that I tried to forget that city. I told myself that I would never come back. I had no idea all this was going on."

"Damn, man. That's a lot . . . a lot to process. You were the head of The Guardian's Army. The strongest out of all of us. That doesn't make sense that he would tell you to stay away."

"I know."

The large creature returns, roaring from the hallway to interrupt all activity in the cells. The slim man follows, tapping his copper collar with his index finger.

"So, sinner – are you ready to confess to your wrong doings?"

"Fuck you," Kinth replies.

You Don't Look Like Us

THE TURN OF THE WIND SLOWS AROUND THE GUARDIAN'S ESTATE as a quiet falls over the Pines. Small signs of peace that often times can be misleading.

If only the quiet lasted.

The city's noise has dulled as the effort to find the human slowly comes to an end for the moment. He wasn't there. The only sounds are created by the wildlife whose echoes sporadically bounce against the trees and the walls around the city.

The next night cycle is creeping in. The only means to visibility around Guardian's Grove is from the indistinct glow from Hock and the security floodlights at various points around the mansion's perimeter. These lights, as well as the dimness of distant-glowing flames. These flames were created by the various people who need to keep warm from the desert chill outside the walls.

The Guardian awakens from his nap and slowly stands to his feet. He stumbles a bit as he takes steps toward the window, gazing out of it once more. He takes another big gulp of wine which had been left on his desk while the last remnant of the desert leaf fizzled away. He replayed the heated conversation he had with the Mantis.

He then approaches a nearby closet, holding the palm of his hand open in front of a scanner. The scanner reads the strategically placed, embedded lines in his skin before beeping. A latch clicks and the closet doors fold outward, revealing a path to another room.

The room contains various items including tactical attire and weapons in near mint condition: HeatMods, M14-NervaToxins, and older, vintage weapons. On an adjacent shelf are various types of canned and dried foods, stacked and organized by name.

The Guardian stares at the display of goods, eyeing one of the canned meals relentlessly; beans he had been saving for quite some time for which he was in no hurry to enjoy. He bites into the can reluctantly, cracking the top of it open without struggle. He tilts his head back, devouring the beans in practically one gulp, before directing his attention to the garments folded on a shelf. Rubbing the stack of clothing with his hand, he grabs a camouflaged uniform, boots and hat.

He checks over his shoulder before sliding a tall painting positioned on the wall to the right. Behind the painting is another door. He turns the knob and opens it, slowly walking down a few levels of winding steps to another section of the mansion.

At the opening to the secret area, he stands perfectly still while studying and admiring the room in the dark. He places his hand on a string connected to a series of lights above him, just before he hears the muffled sound of footsteps upstairs. He then jolts around and runs up the steps quickly.

"Sir. Sir?" The Mantis scans the main room as he walks in.

The Guardian, out of breath, quickly closes the second door, slides the painting back and finishes dressing. He grabs some of the food from the shelf and exits the closet. "I'm coming! I'm coming." The doors of the closet fold inward behind him as he steps back into the main room.

"What were you doing?" The Mantis asks.

The Guardian looks at The Mantis smugly, but doesn't acknowledge the question. "Are we ready?"

"Yes. I have gathered the UG unit for tunnel travel."

"No."

"*No?*"

"We have a stop to make. And we can only make it above ground," The Guardian asserts.

"Is this the reason why you felt the need to put on that?" The Mantis intentionally nods his head forward after folding his arms.

The Guardian gives the Mantis a straight-faced stare. "Can never be too careful."

"As you wish." The Mantis quietly walks out of the room. "Your unit is waiting for you in the rear. I will be in the city. Someone has to stay around and clean up this mess."

The Guardian, annoyed by a number of things, clenches his jaw as he zips up his desert outerwear. He watches the Mantis exits, grabbing a backpack which had been resting beside his desk. Packing the food from his closet along with several pre-rolled desert leafs and multiple bottles of wine, he adds in a pad that was stored within a desk drawer. He looks at Langston's watch once more before stuffing it into one of the smaller pockets of the backpack.

In the rear of the mansion awaits a small group of The Guardian's security. Tired and bewildered, they lounge around, while waiting on their assignment. The Mantis approaches them slowly.

"The Guardian is on his way down. You will be providing him with an escort to Fetela. He wishes to travel above ground, so my suggestion is to stay alert. Use your abilities only when necessary. Otherwise, stick to your weapon of choice. "

The unit's members look at each other, puzzled about the information. The Mantis starts to walk away just as the unit's sergeant suddenly grabs him by the arm. "Above ground? We weren't informed of this. None of my team is prepared for this mission. We need-"

"*Stay . . . alert,*" The Mantis asserts, snatching his arm away. "If you have an issue with these orders, speak to your *leader . . .* about it."

Moments later, The Guardian strolls down the rear steps toward the group. All are still positioned near the back gate, which is different from the others around the city. It has the same design, but it is also equipped with an extra layer of security. Hidden cameras are positioned in each corner and within the set of gate doors is a mantrap.

The Guardian says nothing to the unit as he approaches them. Instead, he eyes them closely, inspecting their weaponry and attire. But more importantly . . . their eyes.

He moves through this inspection briskly, continuing towards the gate, motioning his hand to another set of guards. These guards stand multiple flights up on a platform, manning the gate controls. They pace back and forth, looking over the walls out into the Pines, as well as the activities around The Guardian's estate.

The Guardian twirls his finger and the first gate opens, allowing the group into the mantrap. The group walks in and stands perfectly still while the walls around them close them inward. A blue light activates, steadily moving around them. The light fades before the walls retract and the final gate is opened.

The Guardian remains silent, walking through the gate assertively before they are completely opened. His straight-faced, expressionless demeanor says more than any words can at the moment; a man with many questions, amongst his frustration. A man on a path to seek answers.

The group walks away from the gate silently while strategically spreading out from one another to avoid appearing as one unit to the passersby.

The roads are similar to most of the others around the city: dilapidated and congested due to the remains of business and homes, car parts and trash. All are relics of many things, including sometimes . . . people. At times, people die naturally from the dehydration and starvation; other times, death for any apparent reason. Because of these reasons, it seems as if many people have given up; and the roads showed it.

The heart of the Pines is busier than usual. People are out, walking the streets and talking ecstatically to one another. It is an odd sight to see because of the night which has almost bled into the sky completely.

"You – find out what's going on," The Guardian orders one of his men. "Matter of fact, all of you - find out what has happened. Find out something. Put your weapons away, but stay alert. Try to blend in."

The group nods before spreading out more than before, walking between the makeshift homes and businesses. They listen to everything being said amongst the locals, while blending in as much as possible.

Despite The Guardian's instructions, some of his men walk aggressively through the town. They toss around peoples' belongings and forcefully ask questions about the crowd.

"Hey, you there – why are there so many people out? Why aren't you in your homes?" One of the guards interrupts a nearby conversation between some teens. The youngsters grow nervous and do not respond, quickly dispersing into various directions. They throw random objects at the guard to assist in their getaway. One of the teens trips while trying to double back to pick something up that they dropped. As a result, the guard quickly grabs her by the arm. "Hey; hey. Why are you running? What's happened here?"

"Get off me! Get off me!" the girls screams, causing other people around the altercation to take notice. She struggles to break free, hitting and kicking the guard.

"What do you want with the girl?" A random man shouts from several feet away. His question causes other locals to gather around, wanting to know the same.

The guard releases his grasp. "Nothing. I'm just passing through. Wanted to know what was going on. Never seen so many of y'all out at nightfall. Aren't you afraid of the night lurkers?"

The girl grabs her things while the guard is distracted.

The man studies the guard for a moment. The other locals begin to form a tighter circle around the two. The Guardian overhears the commotion. Approaching slowly, he watches from the distance. He covers his face with the scarf around his neck.

"Are you with them?" the man replies. "We have never seen you in these parts. You don't look like us."

"With who? Who you talkin' 'bout?"

"Them!"

"Them who?" The guard quickly gathers himself and takes a new strategy. "Look - I've been sent from the city to investigate what has happened here. Security near the gates saw the activity."

The man examines the guard's demeanor more before responding. "There was violence at the Exchange. It was upsetting, to say the least. The people here are unnerved."

"But you people are always committing acts of violence against one another. What was so different this time?"

"Everyone! Please! Go back into your homes. Please." The man speaks to the other Pineville citizens before turning his attention back to The Guardian's guard. "Whatever has happened inside those walls has come out to us. Between what we already have to deal with and this new threat; the people here are bothered. Don't you understand? Some of the locals were harmed."

The people begin to dismantle, slowly walking into their homes.

"Harmed by who?" the guard inquires.

"That's just the thing. No one knows who these people were. All we know is that they questioned some of the locals, and ransacked some of the vendor tables before leaving. They took things we have worked hard to attain."

The Guardian looks around before approaching his man and the local. Frustrated, he grows impatient with what he hears. So, he confronts the local, grabbing him by the throat and pushing him against a wall.

"How many were there?" The Guardian's eyes flicker.

"I don't know! I don't know! Two! Three! I didn't see them myself!"

"Which way did they go?"

The man struggles to breathe, grabbing at the arm of The Guardian.

"They – they went North." The teen girl speaks from behind the group, cocking the hammer on a lever action, .22 rifle. "Let my father go," she adds calmly.

"Easy, young lady. No need for that." The Guardian turns his attention back to the man, "North, you say?"

"Yes, North."

The Guardian reaches deep to calm his frustrations, forming a villainous smile. He slowly lets go of the man and walks away with his hands up, because the teenage girl was not budging. He whistles and his entourage gathers around him, weapons drawn.

The Pineville man grabs his throat and coughs as he runs towards his daughter. The two of them quickly exit the area.

The Guardian walks briskly into the dark and climbs a large rock, staring out into the desert night. He pulls out one of the bottles of wine and takes a quick gulp. "That human has been here. There is only one person that can tell me where he is headed." He then jumps down and storms by his men, shoving them out of the way as he continues walking north.

Several roads north - far enough away from the violence and pillaging - in a once quaint and quiet neighborhood - Uncle gathers himself in his library. He meditates while rubbing his arms and neck to sooth the pain which had been inflicted upon him by the strangers. The bounty hunters didn't seem to care who they hurt, just as long as they got what they wanted.

He hobbles into a nearby bedroom and sits slowly, grunting because of the pain in his joints. He is getting older, having aged a little more since the last time he used his abilities. "Wretchedness," He says aloud while grabbing a box of matches sitting on an end table and next to a candle. He strikes one of the matches and lights the candle, holding it close enough to his nose to smell the sweet aroma.

He then grabs a kettle from beside the candle and holds it over the flame. After a minute or two, he takes the kettle and pours himself a drink. He enjoys the taste of a tea, like most other things that he enjoyed, had become scarce. He begins to feel better.

He then strides to his closet, moving some of his belongings aside as he reaches for the box he had retrieved just a few cycles before. He looks through the same photos he had before but reaches deeper in the stack in search for something new this time.

In a manila folder are several documents, similar to the documents Pearl had found in The Guardian's cellar. But the documents he has have more detail. On one of the papers is a handwritten title: UHMUN-DRA; with more words written underneath which say: Human - Designated Residential Area (DRA).

Uncle quickly closes the folder and then the box, putting the box into a vintage briefcase. He drinks the remainder of the tea and puts on a coat, looking around his home before heading toward the rear exit. He pauses for a moment before grabbing a pad and a pencil from the kitchen drawer. Sighing, he writes something on the paper before leaving his home.

Sometime later, The Guardian arrives to his uncle's neighborhood. He motions for his unit to hold their positions and keep a look out.

He then walks slowly toward his uncle's home, reminiscing on how the neighborhood looked many cycles before this moment; a time when all the homes were solid and complete. The shrubbery had been blossoming. The trees stood tall and the smell of a freshly cooked meal filled the air.

He approaches the front door cautiously, smirking to himself.

"Oh, Uncle – guess who," he sings aloud. "Uncle? Come out, you cantankerous, old fool! I have been waiting to use that word on you! Like it?! Uncle?"

Channel Your Abilities

LANGSTON DOESN'T KNOW WHAT TO FEEL; better yet, how to feel. He seems motivated on one hand; the Desert Dwellers were not attacking him as once before. Instead, they were helping him. One extreme has been replaced with another.

Although he knows now what their actual name is – the Ekladi people - they will forever be branded in his mind as the Desert Dwellers or the sand people; the people who had him suspended in the air by his throat. People who used their abilities to blend in with their surroundings and to create clones of themselves.

Is this a trap? Did they have their own agenda which now included him? He thinks these things while chewing gently on his lip, a habit he had formed since a kid. It arose whenever he was nervous or deep in thought.

Either way, he was alive and in the sand people's midst, making his way to hopefully . . . home.

He and Jesse walk in the middle of the large caravan of Ekladi citizens. Despite the size, they form a tight group which looks like a desert creature from the distance. They walk in unison, some using their abilities when necessary to fend off the real desert creatures. Wild birds circle the air, hoping that someone will slack off and drift behind. Traveling solo when these birds are out is not recommended.

Jesse is content for the moment. He has found a new friend, a slightly older girl than he from what he can tell. She has the same abilities that he possesses. He and his new friend walk together, taking turns to use their abilities to impress the other. He smiles a wide smile, one that Langston hadn't seen until this innocent moment. A smile that Jesse himself hadn't had the urge to provide in a long time.

Langston walks near Kira, who decided that she would join the caravan for part of the way. She walks with her arms crossed, and what seems to be a content smile on her face as well. Her skin seems to glow; the slight skylight reflecting off of it. Her long, intricate robe drags the ground behind her. She looks at Langston, noticing the uncertainty in his face.

"My people are disciplined, Langston. I hope you understand this. The incident between us before was not to harm you only for the sake of harming you. We have to assume the worst about whomever we come in contact with." Kira pauses before continuing, "Most of us were once regular people of the Pines, as you probably have experienced. Struggling to survive; operating based on an every-person-for-himself strategy. Gradually, we formed our own set of rules and values. We gravitated away from the negative energy that came from that city. We have to protect what we are building."

"Yeah, I get it. Gotta do what you gotta do," Langston replies, still a bit skeptical.

"We have become who we are, because we help others. One cannot rise unless he helps another rise first," Kira adds. "But, I hope that you find your way and find the answers you seek. You seem to be a good person, Langston. Good people are hard to find. Most people we come in contact seem good on the surface, but their souls are in turmoil."

"Thank you," Langston replies, staring deeply at Kira, as if he is looking through her. He then takes a look at Jesse, before looking at their surroundings. The further the group walks, the greener the landscape becomes. More trees begin to show and the air smells different.

The caravan begins to descend up a hill. At the top of the hill is a bridge which stretches beyond normal sight. The bridge is long, narrow and made of strong pinewood and fiber. Long vines and fungus cover its sides, with the vines hanging low, beyond plain sight.

"What – what is that smell?" Langston asks.

"Water," Kira replies.

"Really?"

"Yes. Natural, beautiful water."

"But why are people dying of thirst and using dirty water if better water is here?"

"This water is sacred and protected. Many have tried to gain access to it, but no one has successfully. This bridge . . . this bridge passes over the great body. People use it to collect whatever droplets they can. It is one of the last of the original bridges created within the seven lands. It should lead you in the direction you wish to go," an elder Ekladi man interjects, pacing in front of the bridge's entrance.

"This is where we part ways, Langston. I hope that our escort service repays the debt we acquired by attacking you before. I wish you and your friend all the great things our universe has to offer," Kira says. She turns her attention to Jesse. "You, young sir – don't be afraid to channel your abilities when you need to, but only for good things. Yes?"

"Okay," Jesse replies. He provides another shy smile as he shakes hands with Kira. He then runs over, hugging his new friend awkwardly before walking toward Langston.

The two of them look at one another before glancing back at Kira and her people. They wave one last time before taking steps closer toward the bridge.

Several miles away, Sam and Rahzy have closed in on Madam Pearl and her men. The two groups battle for some time in the open field. The sky lights up from the various blasts and explosions. Nearby, Hock City patrols can hear and see the fight, so they come to hopefully help end it.

After realizing that it's Madam Pearl who's in danger, the patrols join in for an all-out war between the small Hock Army and the two unknown bounty hunters. But despite the size of the Hock City unit, they are no match for the cleverness and abilities of Sam and Rahzy. The two immobilize the unit again, including their additional help.

Despite hiding behind cover, Madam Pearl had been hit by multiple blasts. She laid on her back, coughing up blood. She tried to crawl her way to nearby shelter, crying and mumbling to herself. Sam notices, and snaps the neck of one of her soldiers as he makes his way toward her.

"I'm going to ask you this once! Where is the human?" Sam says, as he stands over Pearl. He yanks her by her hair and turns her over.

"Who are you?!" Pearl asks.

"Never mind who we are. Now . . . where is the human?!"

"I don't know shit about no human! Get away from me, you filthy son of a bitch!" Pearl shouts.

"You do know!" Sam backhands her. "That's why you came out here to see that old man, ain't it?" He points in the opposite direction, breathing heavily. "Yeah, that's right. We saw you."

Pearl spits blood from her mouth, "You in for some deep shit, putting your hands on me. Do you know who I am?"

"I don't give a shit who you are!"

"I'm The Guardian's sister, you assholes!"

A hush falls over the field. It is as if someone has pressed mute on the conversation and the battle at hand. Sam looks at Rahzy and smiles.

"What?" Rahzy is puzzled.

Sam sighs, "Don't you get it? The man that runs that city! This is his sister! His sister! His flesh and blood! All the commotion back there - he is looking for the human, too. And now, we have his sister."

"Oh. Right."

"You understand?"

"My . . . my brother won't help you." Pearl chimes in, feeling regretful after thinking that she might have shared too much.

"Doesn't matter, sweet cheeks. You are our ticket to getting the human . . . regardless."

"But I thought the old man said −"

"Never mind what that old geezer said, Rahzy," Sam snaps before grabbing Pearl by the arm. "Get up! We're going to take a little trip back to your beloved city."

"My brother ain't there!"

"So? We will *wait* for him to return, then."

He's Alive!

THE PRISONERS BEGIN TO GET DISORDERLY AT THE SIGHT OF THE STANDOFF between Kinth and the slim man, better known as Sir Grace.

"IF YOU DON'T REPENT OF YOUR SINS, YOU DO NOT EAT!" Sir Grace yells.

"Well, I guess I'm not eatin,'" Kinth replies.

"Kinth, man – c'mon. You just got in here! Don't do this, please! They goin' move you. C'mon man!" Aldo does his best to persuade his stubborn friend.

"Shh!" The slim man snaps his fingers, responding to Aldo's outburst. He then claps his hands twice rapidly. Three large creatures approach from various parts of the dreary, makeshift prison. The sounds of their bulky, sluggish bodies bounce off the walls. The largest of the three creatures approach Kinth's cell, unlocking it with a special key.

Kinth clenches his teeth as he takes a few steps backwards. His jaw muscles pulsate as he watches the creature open the cell and walk in.

"Last chance, sinner."

"SINNER!" the prisoner across the way screams.

"Shut up!" Aldo yells back. "Oh boy," he whispers to himself before plopping to the floor and covering his face with his hands.

Kinth maintains his silence. He balls his fist at first, preparing for a fight. But then, he opens his hands and holds them up to expose his palms. "*Easy*, big fella. Easy. No need for force. I will go willingly." *More of my men could be where they plan to take me,* he thinks.

The creature grunts and walks toward Kinth intensely. The slim man claps his hands rapidly once more. The creature acknowledges by stopping in its tracks, breathing heavily. Saliva falls from its mouth as it shows its bulky, putrid teeth.

"Does this mean that you are you repenting, sinner?"

"Repent? Noooo. I've been a good boy all my life, Sir Ugly."

The slim man sighs. "I have no time for this. Seize him."

The creature roars loudly before striking Kinth in his face, knocking him unconscious.

"Shit," Aldo says under his breath. "Can we talk about this? He doesn't know the rules yet. None of this is necessary. Please."

"Silence, peasant." Sir Grace replies. "You know where to take him."

The creatures grab Kinth by his legs, dragging him like a ragdoll down an adjoining hallway.

Sounds of screams and wailing begins to wake Kinth. The random voices and sporadic yelps bang on his head like the creature once had just moments before. *The echoes of other sinners who refused to repent,* he presumes.

"PLEASE! PLEASE! I'M STARVING! PLEASE!" One of the prisoners screams, holding his stomach. "PLEASE! FEED ME OR THROW ME OVER! PLEASE!"

"SHUT UP! SHUT UP!" A second prisoner says, just before he begins to punch on the beggar.

After collecting himself, Kinth sits up and leans on a nearby wall. He is in a much larger cell than before. There's little lighting, no windows and no bars; just a solid, block of a room. He observes what he can. He can see the limbs and silhouettes of bodies and faces, but nothing or no one is entirely clear.

"Hey, boy – give me what you got," the prisoner stops beating on the other hungry cellmate, and instead barks an order at Kinth.

Kinth chuckles as he rubs his head. The blow he took from the creature is causing an ache.

"Don't make me tell you again."

"I suggest you move on," Kinth replies.

The prisoner approaches Kinth more, bending down directly in front of him.

"I don't think you understand, boy. I am the top dog in here. People fear me in all parts of the Pines. I am -"

Just before the prisoner can continue his statement, Kinth front kicks him in the groin. It causes the man to squeal and fall backwards. Kinth struggles to his feet. His head is still aching, and he's still a bit dazed. He straddles the man, beginning to pound on him so hard that the man's body cracks the stone beneath him.

Suddenly, a loud roar echoes throughout the space. The roar shakes the cell, frightening everyone but Kinth. Small particles of stone and debris fall from the ceiling. The wide cell door is then opened.

"Enough!" the slim man shouts. His trusty creatures enter the space before he does. "You have only been in here for a short while and are already causing problems I see." He strolls in after his beastly servant, moving slowly in order to witness all the activity.

"No problem here. Just having a talk with a new friend." Kinth pounds the bully once more, knocking him out. Blood flies into the air.

"Enough! That's what you call a talk?"

"Well. You know how some talks can be."

The slim man forms a frustrated smile before walking deeper into the room. "As for the rest of you other worthless beings, your demise is near. Some of you are already shriveling away. Repent and maybe I will extend your life. Maybe even send you back to your people. Or, die in here . . . and become food for my winged friend outside. Or, for my friends here." The slim man rubs the nearest creature with the back of his hand. He says something in quiet before storming out of the room, leaving behind one creature to keep watch.

Kinth stands and stares at his hands. He rubs them together, the blood from the man dripping from his knuckles. He feels a tug on his shirt from behind. Turning around, there is a frail man standing behind him. The man rubs his hands together, struggling to create a small flame in his palms which comes and goes. He checks and then double-checks that the slim man is gone before trying again. The flame enlarges and steadies. The creature notices the flicker of light, but only grunts and turns away. Eventually, he follows behind Sir Grace.

"Please. I mean no harm. Please. Come; come. Come this way. Quickly," the frail man whispers with an accent that Kinth hadn't heard before. He walks away quickly, deeper into the cell behind a set of columns. He uses all his strength to maintain the flame.

Kinth watches the man a little bit. He studies him before reluctantly following him to the back corner of the room. The frail man points to the corner where someone is laying on their side, facing the wall. The person laying down waves for help, while two other prisoners assist in turning the person over to face the others nearby.

The frail man moves more into the corner, so that the light from the flames in his palms can illuminate the area. Kinth watches closely, keeping a stern eye on everything that is happening.

"Kin . . . Kinth. Kinthingson," the man that was once facing the wall struggles to speak.

Kinth has become frozen in his steps. He feels like someone has sucked the air out of the room. He can't seem to catch his breath or form a word. His eyes feel like they are swelling, with a river of tears forming behind a dam that's ready to give way.

"Father?"

"Kinthingson, come. Come to me."

Kinth falls to his knees. He feels emotions that he hadn't felt in ages; feelings that causes his eyes to well up with tears. He crawls toward his father. His mouth moves slightly, but without words. He attempts to say something more, but he can't. One tear forms and gradually slides down his face like droplets on a window.

"Father?" he says again, his voice weakened.

"Yes, son. Please, come closer."

Kinth's father - the original Guardian and one of the founding fathers of Pineville; the once praised leader of Hock City. He is alive! Alive! But not well. He is just as frail – if not more – than the nearby prisoner who illuminates the area with flames within his palms.

The once tall, burly leader – who once had a lush beard and head full of hair - is now a thin, expressionless man. His beard is sparse and his hair is thinning. His muscles are dwindling. He has aged greatly with each day that he has been locked away.

"Please, help me up," Father says.

Kinth and other random prisoners rush to his side and help the feeble elder up. He then rests his back against a wall.

"I – I don't understand. I thought you were dead. I thought –"

"Listen. We don't have much time. He will return soon –"

"The priest?"

"He is not a priest, my son. He is just a . . . troubled man," Father coughs. He speaks again after catching his breath. "Listen to me closely. I need to tell you as much as I can before he returns."

"What is this place?"

"Please. Listen. I will explain as much as I can."

"Okay," Kinth nods before looking over his shoulder. He notices various shadows moving along the walls outside of the cell. Someone is pacing the hallways, probably listening.

A small group of prisoners run toward the gate and pretend to fight, creating a small distraction.

"I know you have many questions, but please just listen for now. I'm sure you are well-aware that your brother has assumed the title as Guardian over the city."

Kinth shakes his head. He looks down, pausing before replying. "Yes."

"For many years, your brother has had the inclination that he wasn't loved; that I didn't adore him like I adore you or your sister. And your mother when she was alive. He has always been in competition with you'll — with anyone — even me; all the way up until he decided to betray me and take over as leader of the city."

"I know. But what happened? When did you know? Why did you send me away? And why did you send messages for me to not return? I was . . . I was hurt." Kinth grabs his father's hand, rubbing his arid skin softly.

"Because I didn't want us both to be in here, son. Like this! The way we are now! I sent you on that mission to hopefully keep you alive. I could see that your brother was not letting up. He challenged me often. I felt a change coming, and I did what I thought was necessary. I followed my instincts. I see that my gut didn't lie! Didn't think that it would get this bad, but . . . my idea partly worked! You are alive! I encouraged your sister to venture out, too. But she was too stubborn. She didn't want to leave, mostly because your brother played on her emotions. And then, not long afterwards, Franklin found out about my plans."

"What plans?"

"My plans to protect and preserve the humans that we had left living in our society. Son, when Hock was first conceived, it was a beautiful place. Despite the events that changed us, we were one people – together without much discord. But everything changed when some of us saw that we had abilities and learned that we could use them with criminal intentions. There was no more peace among us. So, I consulted in private with my counsel and your uncle. I came up with a plan to evacuate the remaining humans to their own area."

"But why?"

"Because we needed them. We were going to study them to figure out a way to use their genetics; to get everyone else human again. To return us to what we truly are. Many of our beloved citizens died because of their abilities; so, so many. I wanted to end that. So I came up with this idea, and I gave the project a name. I only told a few about this."

"What is the name?"

"I called the project 'Uhmandra.'"

"I – I – I'm so confused, Father. Uhmandra?"

"Yes. It was sort of an acronym, but not quite. Just flipped letters, really, with the meaning hidden in plain sight: Human Designated Residential Area. Son, I can't prove it, but I believe our abilities are killing us slowly." Father coughs and wipes his mouth. "Anytime you use one of your gifts, you lessen your lifespan. I haven't been able to prove it but look around you. Close your eyes and look back at some of the people you encountered. Your uncle, Shaida, Franklin, me - people in the city and in Pineville. We have all aged faster than the humans. Once I started to notice this, I began developing my plan."

"This is . . . so much to process. How did you get in here?"

"Your brother, of course. This place was supposed to be a connecting point – another safe haven for our people to pass through. But your brother made a deal with that man. The so-called priest. After he put me here, he began bringing anyone who didn't agree with his leadership here, too."

Kinth listens attentively, clenching his jaw at every mention of his brother. "But who is this Sir Grace person?"

"I don't know. Probably just a lowlife that has a relationship with your brother. Nothing more," Father speaks emphatically.

Shouting ensues in another section of the prison, causing the creatures to move quickly nearby.

"Before I was brought here, I arranged for a place for the humans to go. A safe haven. I consulted with the Land of Longleaf. Longleaf Counsel agreed to designate an area for our humans to live, where they could co-exist without threat. Hidden and in secrecy. Then, I started to go to each home of the humans in Hock, personally but as quiet as I could. I needed them to feel the urgency of my theory. I told each human my beliefs. Some understood and were grateful with my plans to protect them. I hoped to help them rid their family members of their abilities in order to preserve their natural, human state. They saw the importance of living a long, fruitful life. A normal life. Some just wanted out of the city. But, there were many whom were not in agreement. They enjoyed their abilities and what they were able to gain from them. A lot of these people left Hock abruptly, or stayed and sided with your brother.

"Franklin somehow found out about my plans, and he approached me. He told me that life was better with our abilities. He fell in love with the control he gained from the use of his, and spread his sentiments to his friends and others. He refused to support my idea that life would be better for us all, if we were human again. So, he threatened to spread lies about me if I continued my plans. These things happened just after I sent you away."

"Lies? What lies?" Kinth asks.

"I am ashamed to say. But after you left, he started to tell people that I was having affairs with various human women. That I was trying to become human again by interacting inappropriately with these humans. Nonsense; all just plain nonsense. I would never! He said that I was poisoning the beautiful empire of genetically modified people. He spread hate, and hate begets hate. He used this hate to fuel his own campaign to take over."

"This is why Uncle left as well?"

"Yes. Your uncle warned me early on that he felt a negative energy forming around me, even before I announced my plans. He made his own choice to leave the city before the changes, but stayed in touch with me through messenger. Other times I went to see him."

Kinth moves in closer. He grows anxious. "A human has crossed my path. He – he was stranded in the Pines and stumbled across my hideout."

"No one just stumbles on anything, son. The universe always connects us to the next thing we need to grow within our lives. We just have to recognize these things."

"Are you saying . . . you are aware of this human? Did you send this human?"

Father pauses for a moment. "No. But I know that humans aren't treated the same in other lands. So there can be many reasons why this human found you."

"But, but – he is believed to be our kin!" Kinth's voice rises. He checks over his shoulder before continuing. "He thinks he is our brother."

"No, son. You, your sister and brother are the only fruit of my loins. This person – this human - believes this because of the lies your brother has shared with him or someone else. Your brother has made me out to be some sort of – some sort of sexual parasite. This is a lie."

"So where did this human come from? And he's not the only person that has found me in that desert. There have been others."

"I do not know. But you – you can find out!" Father coughs uncontrollably.

A hush falls over the cell, extending to others nearby. Everyone close to the conversation has become absorbed by the story that Father has been telling his concerned son, who he hadn't seen in many cycles.

Kinth looks at his father. He studies his aged skin and recognizes his troubled breathing. He is bothered by how he appears. He is not the strong, solid man he used to be.

"Father, we have to get you outta here. We have to get you food and clean water. Somewhere safe with uncle, so we can figure out a way to put a stop to Franklin's rule."

Father chuckles. "I am old, son. My abilities and this place have taken a toll on me. No man was meant to live in solitude like this."

"No matter, Father! We can do it! I can get you outta here!"

"Shh, shh. Please don't bring any more attention to us. I have seen many taken away. That man out there is just as troubled as your brother. Most of what you see here, he does for sport."

The creatures return to inspect the cell. After seeing nothing of concern, they turn around before exiting toward another hallway.

"Son, I must rest. But, listen to me. Find the human. Find your way to Longleaf and Uhmandra. Everything will make sense there. Continue what I started." Father touches Kinth's face gently.

"Why me? Why do I have to be a part of this? We can get you out and healthy again. You can lead again."

"I love you, son. Trust me. It is your time. Our people's future depends on this." Father lies down on his side. He grabs Kinth's hand. "I must rest. You should rest as well. Everything will be fine. The universe always knows what's best."

Nobody Is Safe

UNCLE WALKS WEARILY INTO THE OPEN DESERT LAND outside of his home. He hastens along - sweat forming on his brow. He hopes to get as far away as he can from the once safe confines of his home, before someone or something picks up on his trail.

He clutches his belongings, doing his best to keep his balance while traversing the lumpy, dry land. He pauses for a moment, turning around to look at his residence from the distance. He feels as though this may be the last time he will see it. And he just might be right. All depends on what the Pines will have in store for him.

After thinking more, he realizes that he doesn't have a plan on where to go. He left his home abruptly, with no real idea on his destination. He thought of getting away as fast as he could, because of the forethought that The Guardian would eventually send for him.

For some time, The Guardian would visit him with the sole intention to use his uncle's abilities for his own gain. Because of this, and other reasons, he didn't want any parts of his nephew. Nor any parts of the evils of the city.

Uncle has been walking for a while. His body began to shiver as the wind picks up and the temperature drops. He must make a decision quickly about traveling any further, because he is not equipped to deal with the desert at night.

He reaches deep into his pocket, pulling out a cinnamon-flavored throat lozenge and tossing it into his mouth. The spicy flavor warms him at the same time opening his sinuses. He starts to blow his nose but decides to wipe it instead. He can't afford to make any unnecessary noises during his journey.

He sighs and mumbles to himself as he takes another step. He keeps walking, using his abilities when he feels strong enough to create a cloak around him. The cloak provides a protective camouflage layer, but only in short increments. Using his abilities any longer than a few moments would surely incapacitate him.

He begins to feel something brewing within him. A voice tells him to alter his path. He changes directions, heading towards the old gas station in which Kinth once dwelled. The area was practically deserted, which was one of the main reasons Kinth probably chose to settle there. So what was left for Uncle to find?

"Oh, alright! Alright," he thinks aloud.

He presses forward toward the outskirts of Hock City. A slight change in course that leads him to the part of the Pines in which Langston said he was found. The light of the sky begins to darken before he can make good ground; so, he chooses to venture to safe grounds and to the nearest watering hole available. He hadn't had a drink in some time.

He notices the flicker of a fire a ways ahead, so he journeys in that direction. Meanwhile, he stumbles onto a group of people sitting in lawn chairs around a barrel that houses a flame. They are huddled together, some with blankets to keep warm.

"Uh – excuse me, fellows. Can you point me to the nearest brewery? I am in need of a drink," Uncle asks hesitantly. Uncle's request is met with only silence. He begins to turn away and keeps walking but elects to try speaking to the group once more. "I say, please –"

"Get outta here, you uppity old fool. Nobody in these parts talk like you," one of the men says, interrupting the request with a brusque tone. He mumbles more of this sentiment under his breath.

"Please, sir. I promise you that I am not . . . uppity, as you call it. I just want to rid my thirst."

"You have anything to trade, old man?" another member of the group asks. He throws a sharp compact axe at the ground, killing a rattlesnake without looking.

"I –" Uncle grows somewhat nervous.

Before he can continue his response, another man walks up and sits with the group. He wears a skullcap and a vintage leather jacket, paired with cargo pants and old sneakers. "C'mon now. Don't treat the man like this. That's not what we are about." The man then directs his attention to the newcomer. "Here. Have a seat. I have some ale," he adds.

"Don't give that man our ale, Jack! We don't know who he is?!"

"Oh shut up, Nelson! Haven't we all had enough bullshit today? Can't we just enjoy some ale in peace with a potential new friend?!"

"But look what happened the last time strangers passed through here?! They attacked Eli!"

As the two locals debate, Uncle feels faint and sits in the only available chair. He closes his eyes and meditates, beginning to see the events that happened at the Exchange. Although, he can't quite make out the faces. He concentrates harder, but almost falls out of the chair, winded. One of the locals rushes to his aid.

"You alright, mister?"

"Yes. Yes. Thank you. Just a little lightheaded. Been traveling for quite some time." Uncle straightens his shirt, embarrassed. "I'm sorry, but I don't mean to pry. But did you say there was an attack?"

"You ain't with them - are you, mister?"

"No. No. I promise you I'm not."

The locals study Uncle's demeanor a bit more before speaking again. "Some strangers came through our Exchange not too long ago. They weren't from round here. Like ten of 'em!"

"It wasn't no damn ten, Willy!" another local chimes in.

"Whatever! They had on some strange clothing. One of 'em looked like he had some different abilities than I ever seen before. They asked one of our buddies some questions and then roughed him up."

"What did they want to know?"

"Somethin' bout a human!" another local yelps.

"Enough!" the apparent leader of the group interrupts. "Y'all talk too damn much!"

"I'm sorry. I didn't mean to pry," Uncle says, calmly.

"What are you doing in these parts?"

Uncle thinks for a moment, planning his responses carefully, "I believe those men might have started their roughhousing in the city. I didn't want any parts of that so I am traveling to see family until whatever is going on comes to an end."

"I don't blame ya. Family, you say?"

"Yes, sir."

"Where is your family?"

"Not too far away. In the outskirts - like here. But they don't frequent this area."

"Hmph. Here. Drink," the leader takes a sip of ale and passes the cup to Uncle. He watches as Uncle takes a sip also.

"Thank you." Uncle drinks a large portion before belching.

"Ah, well look at that! The old fart can hold his liquor!" Willy says.

"I've had my share!" Uncle laughs.

The group chuckles before most of them become silent. Uncle stares at the ground and thinks, while some of the others eventually begin talking quietly amongst themselves.

"You eat rattlesnake?" the leader asks.

"Not in some time. I have grown accustom to eating less meat with my age."

"Well, if you change your mind, we goin' roast that one in a bit."

"Thank you kindly."

Another awkward moment of silence occurs. The leader talks to his friends before turning his attention back to the elderly visitor. "I don't know what's going on, but something odd is happening behind those walls and up past those hills." The leader leans toward Uncle, pointing in the opposite direction.

"What do you mean?"

The leader stands. "Take a walk with me." He begins to stroll into the connecting neighborhood of crude homes and businesses, waving at the few who were still outside. "I must admit that I am just as suspicious as my friends back there. They have a point. You don't talk like us. And shit, you don't even smell like us. But we are peaceful folk, so you don't have to worry. Not about me, anyway. I must say, though . . . I am curious to know why you decided to stop here. You may appear an old man, but you may *not* be an old man. Catch my drift?"

"I assure you, kind sir. I am an old man. I do have abilities but nothing worth much. I came only for a drink. "

"What can you do?"

The old man closes his eyes and makes an empty bucket nearby slide across the ground. He then stumbles down one knee, pretending to be winded again.

"Impressive."

"Yes, but with my age this skill is limited. But . . . "

"But?"

"After hearing what your fellows said, I hope to learn anything you wish to share," Uncle states calmly.

"About?"

"Why did you hush the young man when he mentioned a human?"

The local sighs. "I have heard stories about the humans. The people who know too much of these stories are eventually never see again. So, let's just say I like for me and mines to stay quiet. It's the best thing for us to do. Understand?"

"I understand. But if you can share any information, I promise you I will leave. And you will never see me again. Nor will anyone come here and bother you because of me. I, too, come from peaceful people. And I just want to protect my family in the same fashion."

The local stares at the elderly stranger, maintaining eye contact for an intensely long moment. He observes his surroundings before taking a step closer so that he can whisper.

"Usually, a person would have to make a trade to gain anything in these parts, even information. But, for you . . ." The local takes out a large Bowie knife. He rotates the blade to show it off, before making a long cut into the palm of his hands. Yellowy blood begins to flow into his palm ". . . I can make an exception."

Uncle looks down at the local's hand. He frowns a little, shaking his head before holding his hand out. *This is not what I expected,* he thinks. The local makes the same incision on the elder's hand, with the same yellowy blood forming in his palms. The two shake, causing the blood to drip from their palms onto the dry, desert soil.

The local then sits on a bench. He reaches into his pocket, grabbing a cloth. "Here."

"Thank you." Uncle takes the cloth and wraps it around his hand.

"Listen. All I can tell you is - the humans are being killed off. One by one. Either that, or taken away."

"Taken away? Where?"

"That I don't know. What I do know is that, somewhere in Dyadika, they are doing something to the humans."

"Doing what?"

"I don't know. Whatever they are doing, it isn't working. The humans are dying. They are dumping the bodies not far from here."

"How do you know this?"

"Look at us. We scavenge. We wander. We search and move around for our survival. Some time ago, one of our friends went missing. We think he stumbled onto where they are dumping the bodies."

Uncle pauses before replying. "I'm sorry about your friend."

"Yeah. We miss him." The local clears his throat, clearly saddened by the moment. "Some sick fucks are doing something to those poor people. The women and the old folk. Just sick! And the people with abilities, too. Nobody is safe."

Uncle listens attentively to what the local has to say. As he listens, he reaches into his belongings to find something worthy to trade for the information. *It's only right to give him something,* he thinks. A bloody handshake didn't seem enough. He grabs a small, clear sandwich bag that contains seeds.

"Well, I do thank you for your hospitality and for your time," Uncle says, as he rattles the seeds in front of him.

"What's this?"

"I'm sure sustenance is hard to come by for you and your family, so here are some seeds to grow tomatoes."

The local takes the bag, looks at it and tosses it back. "Nothing is growing out here. Too dry."

"On the contrary, sir, these tomatoes will grow easily."

"How are you so sure?"

"Trust me. They will."

Fetela

THE GUARDIAN WALKS AGRESSIVELY THROUGH HIS UNCLE'S HOME. He storms from one end of the vintage dwelling to the other - up and down the stairs, breathing heavily, and leaving soiled footprints on the floors. He opens and slams doors, ripping some from their hinges.

He can tell that his uncle has been there recently by the scent of pipe smoke in the air; this as well as the understanding that his uncle rarely leaves the home. But his uncle is not there. And so, The Guardian grows further frustrated, throwing his elderly kin's belongings around to find any clues on where he may be headed. *What would make him leave?* The Guardian thinks, growing further suspicious.

"I know you're in here, you old bastard! Come out!" The Guardian shouts, speaking harshly into the air as he stands in the kitchen. His order is met with silence. He waits, thinking that his uncle would eventually oblige, but still – nothing.

The Guardian hums to himself before grabbing one of the many walnuts from a bowl on the kitchen counter. He cracks it with one hand and tosses the broken nuts into his mouth. He chews insistently before speaking again. "Okay, Uncle. I will be back. Trust that I will. And when I do . . . we will have a much need talk."

He then storms outside, motioning to his men to fall in to his location. He doesn't provide any update on what happened in his uncle's home, as his men gather together. Instead, he just presses forward to his original planned destination. By the expression on his face, The Guardian's men ask no questions and willingly follow.

The group travels for some time – even through the cycle of darkness. They traverse the desert hills and valleys; climbing the rough, manmade roads on the sides of mountains. Expeditiously, they keep moving until they see a large, inoperable Ferris wheel ahead. The Ferris wheel meant they were at the edge of Fetela, another city within the Pines. The Ferris wheel sits behind private security fencing forming a wide square, enclosing various tall buildings, smaller stores and the remains of a boardwalk.

There is no water beneath or near the wooden structure – just more sand and soil. There are no people around, except for armed guards standing at alert.

The guards are perched in several of the Ferris wheel seats, keeping an eye on all the terrain around the fenced community. A large beast, wearing dark linen with leather straps positioned as a belt and holster, manually turns the wheel. With each turn, it positions a new guard at the top of the wheel to share the lookout duties.

One of the guards recognizes The Guardian and his entourage as he approaches. "That's far enough, *Franklin*," the large Tarantulan guard says.

"That's The Guardian to you – you crazy-eyed beast."

"What do you want? Why are you here?" The guard speaks in a cold tone.

"I need to speak with Mathias."

"Mathias is done in his dealings with you," the guard snaps back, widening his other set of legs aggressively. He jumps down to a lower seat on the wheel, seething.

"Since when do you speak for him?" The Guardian continues to approach the entrance, disregarding the sentiments of the armed creature.

Suddenly, the other guards on the wheel fire an array of bullets horizontally at the ground a few feet from where The Guardian walks. Sand flies into the air. The Guardian stops, grunting at the threat of force and snapping his fingers. His men draw their weapons, ready for an all-out fire fight.

"Stop! We do not waste ammunition! How many times do I have to say this?! What is going on out here?" Mathias yells some yards away inside the fence, as he walks up to the guarded entrance. He peaks through an opening in the gate and notices The Guardian. "Oh boy. You again? Still making trouble everywhere you plant your feet, I see."

"Mathias!" The Guardian sings. "My old trader-friend. How art thou?"

"Save me your bullshit, Franklin. What do you want?"

"Why do I have to want something? Why can't I just stop by to say hello?"

"Shoot him," Mathias says to one of his men. Mathias's security lifts, activating their weapons.

"Okay, okay, okay. Relax, relax. Tell them to relax."

"No time for your bullshit, Franklin. I have much work to tend to. I am a very busy."

"No bullshit, I promise."

"You only come here when you want something. I am a trader, but I have my limits. My patience-"

"I know, I know," The Guardian interrupts. "I just want to know what you did with those . . . *care packages*."

Mathias squints, eyeing The Guardian closely before responding, "Let this annoyance in. But your group must wait here. Check him for weapons. And if you interrupt me again, I will kill you myself."

"Guardian, sir. I don't advise —"

"It's okay. It's okay," The Guardian calms his guard. He approaches the gate where he is inspected. He delivers a smug expression to the Tarantulan standing on the wheel, scratching the side of his face with his middle finger. "Mathias! It's good to see you!" he says.

Mathias is roughly six feet tall, with a narrow jaw and a third eye above the two others. He has two teeth, hanging slightly outside of his mouth. His head is shaven on the sides with tattoos covering most of his scalp.

Mathias sucks his teeth and turns around, walking quickly to a nearby bench that is positioned in front of a once functional ice cream store.

"Why are you here, Franklin?"

"What have you been doing with the humans?"

"Shh, keep your voice down."

"Keep my voice down? Why? There is no one out here really," The Guardian looks around, taking his bag and placing it in his lap.

"There is always someone out here. My people are quiet but observant. I like to think that I know the city that I lead."

"Whatever you say, man." The Guardian reaches into his bag and pulls out a flask. He takes a sip of ale and offers Mathias some.

"No, thanks."

"So? The humans?"

"What about them?"

"What did you do with them?"

"I'm a trader. What do you think I did with them?"

"What?! That wasn't our deal."

"Our deal," Mathias chuckles. "Our deal was more like a favor. One that was only beneficial to you. I took on more mouths than I could feed all so that you can take over a once pleasant city and run it into the ground."

"Watch your tongue, friend."

"Don't bark orders at me in my city!" Mathias stands to his feet abruptly.

"And by the same token, don't assume you know anything about my plans for *my* city." The Guardian responds, coolly.

"Is that not what you have done? My people say that your locals run your city more than you do."

The Guardian does his best to withhold his first thought, thereby avoiding going toe-to-toe within an unpleasant debate. Especially as he sits alone and unarmed in Mathias's presence. "Look. Our deal was that I provide you with workers and you provide me with technology and weapons!"

"Yes, but our *deal* was voided when you failed to tell me that your workers were human," Mathias replies, sitting down on the bench.

Mantis, The Guardian thinks. "Well, clearly my instructions were not followed as I insisted. You should have known that I would never try to hide something like this from you during a trade. My apologies for this."

"Do you realize how close I came to my people finding out? To having them turn against me for using our already thin resources to protect humans? I lead with transparency. If someone here had of discovered there were humans amongst us, there would have been a rebellion! I could have lost all that I built."

"I get it. I get it. I apologized. What more do you want me to say?"

Mathias looks away, studying the streets and watching some of his people move around in the distance.

"Just tell me . . . who has the humans now? And I will be out of your hair," The Guardian continues. "Trust me. I don't like visiting this place more than I have to anyway."

"Like everything else, the humans were traded – but done so privately."

"To who?"

"That information you are not privy to. My business with you is done."

"But I need to know, Mathias!"

Mathias stands and whistles toward the gated entrance. A few of his guards approach. "Please see this gentlemen out, and if you see him again, you have my authority to kill him on-sight."

The Guardian walks toward the entrance in front of Mathias's men. He stops suddenly and turns around, "Till we meet again, friend."

Mathias begins to boil with rage in the distance.

The Great Escape

KINTH IS HAVING TROUBLING SLEEPING. He isn't used to sharing his space with anyone, especially noisy strangers in a cold cell. But they all aren't strangers. It has been many cycles since he last saw his father, so he uses the little silence between the shouting to stare at the much older likeness of himself.

His father is physically much different now compared to when he saw him last. As a kid, he remembers seeing a strong man who used to sling an axe effortlessly at their home, splitting wood without taking a second wind. What he sees of his father now bothers him greatly.

He continues to rests near him, propped against the wall. He watches over him like a mother bird watching over her nest. Yet, he watches over him the same way his father did for him when he caught a cold as a child. The roles seem reversed as his father struggles to sleep, his breathing growing weaker by the minute. He grabs at his stomach while he rests, apparently trying to fight the hunger that feels as though it is trying to tear its way out of him.

Kinth grows even more frustrated while watching his father struggle. No one should endure the type of pain that he believes the people in this cell has endured, especially his own family. He thinks deeply, trying to calm the rage that is growing inside him.

He hops to his feet and storms to the cell door, shouting, "Can someone please give the old in here some food?! Please! At least the old should eat!" No one responds. Kinth, feeling deflated, repeats himself, but still there's no response.

"I know that scar." Someone whispers from the corner, pulling Kinth's attention away from his unheard demands. "I remember it well. I remember you and your father."

Kinth turns his attention toward the voice. He notices a man, older but not quite the age of his father, sitting against the wall. He is like many of the others in the room, half naked with scraps of cloths covering the private areas of his body. He has circles of various designs branded all over his chest and arms.

The man continues. "I remember when my mother first brought us into the city; your father ruled. We were poor, and he showed us mercy. He let us inside – any of us, as long as we were willing to contribute to the growth of the city. I can't say that I have seen too many leaders like that. But what do I know? I don't remember much of you, other than seeing you by his side often."

Kinth looks the man over for a minute before saying anything; a bit of an uncomfortable silence. "What is your name, friend?" he finally says, kneeling down beside the man.

"Enrico. Most people just call me Rico. I don't know what this place is, but a bunch of us were brought here some time ago."

"Why?"

Enrico sucks his teeth. "If you didn't agree with the rules or if you weren't supposed to be in the city to begin with, you were brought here. And others like my family, who didn't have the lines to pay to stay – well . . . you understand."

Kinth ensures nobody is listening before responding, "Are you – are you . . . human?" he whispers.

"No, no. I couldn't tell you what a human looks like to save my life. Only heard stories. I have abilities. Everyone in here has some sort of ability. Some more useful than others."

"What can you do?"

"Not much anymore. But I can do this . . ." The man struggles to stand, leaning on Kinth to get his balance. He exhales deeply before he extends his hands. His body trembles deeply as he wiggles his fingers. The motion creates a visual copy of the people and the wall nearby. "I used to be able to recreate whatever I could imagine. Now I can only create a copy of what's in front of me. For some reason – I just don't feel strong like I used to."

Kinth walks around and inspects the visual Enrico produces. It was as if a projector had been placed in the room, and it was displaying a copy of what Kinth could see in the air. "Impressive. Save your strength, friend. We will need it," he replies.

Enrico swallows deeply, "Need it? What are you talkin' about?"

"I have a plan to get us outta here."

Enrico chuckles as he returns to his seat. "There is no way *outta* here."

"There is always a way. If you want to see your family again, trust me. Would you rather sit here and wither away, or at least die trying to get back to your family?"

The man looks at Kinth, the same way Kinth looked at him just moments before. He then nods at Kinth's sentiments.

A great distance away, Langston and Jesse begin to slowly cross the aging bridge. Jesse plays with the vines, hanging around it, swinging them back and forth as they pass. He wonders how strong the vines are, and if he wanted to hang from one. *Better not,* he thinks after tugging on a longer, slightly loose piece of it.

The bridge hangs between large, moist, moss-covered stone. The mist-filled air almost feels like light rain falling. Jesse arches his head up and holds out his tongue, attempting to taste the condensation. Langston smiles, feeling at peace for the first time in a while.

Suddenly, Langston's body jerks and tightens causes him to fall on one knee. His eyes seem to roll back in his head. He groans in slight anguish as he drifts backwards against one of the bridge columns, practically falling from the edge. Once more his body jerks as his thoughts move rapidly. He grabs at his arms, scratching at his skin as if to remove something.

He yells out, "No, no! No more! Please! No more!"

"Mr. Langston! Mr. Langston!" Jesse exclaims, running to his side to grab him. He pulls him as hard as he can away from the edge.

Langston's body uncontrollably shakes for a few more seconds before stopping. He breathes heavily as he blinks his eyes. He looks over at Jesse, who appears stunned as he quivers at what he is seeing.

"Wha - what happened?" Langston asks.

"I don't know! You just – just fell and started actin' weird!"

Langston pulls himself up using the bridge's guard rope to sit. He rubs his face and head to gather himself but is still quite not with his bearings. "Where's my watch? Where's my watch?" Langston adds, nervously.

"Huh?"

Langston groans and squints his eyes, doing his best to get himself together. He inspects his arms again.

"Are you okay?" Jesse asks.

"I – I don't know. I guess. I felt . . . like – it felt like a sharp pain. Couldn't control it. Felt like . . . I don't know. Man, that was odd."

"Like what?"

"Let's just keep going."

Jesse helps Langston to his feet. "You screamed some stuff, too."

"What did I say?"

"You just kept saying 'no,' and some other stuff."

Langston looks at Jesse, as if he is expecting more of an explanation. He shakes his head before walking away in the same direction as they started. "Can't remember much. I just felt like something had me by my arms. Like I was strapped down to something. And then I felt a sharp pain. Let's get across this bridge. Hopefully there is somewhere safe where we can rest. Maybe I just need some water."

Jesse listens, but doesn't have much to add. This part of the conversation ends for the moment as the two continue to walk the course of the bridge. The bridge design turns as it goes upward, shaking some with the shift in weight which the two travelers place on it. The old planks groan with each step.

"I wonder if Miles is okay," Jesse says randomly, sounding troubled.

"He seems like the type of guy where not much fazes him," Langston says after taking some time to gather a response. "Am I right?"

Jesse nods. "Yeah. He has always watched my back, and Madam Pearl's, too. I hope nothin' happened to him."

Langston pats Jesse on the back as a small act of empathy and reassurance. He keeps walking without responding, to avoid dampening the mood. He is still nervous about what just happened to him, and can't recall ever feeling the way he just did.

He stops briefly to look back over his shoulder at how far they have traveled. He can no longer see the desert hills where he and Jesse left Kira and the other Ekladi people. Langston mentally replays everything he was told by Kira and her people.

"Mr. Langston, look!" Jesse exclaims, breaking Langston's eagle-eye gaze in the opposite direction.

Langston turns around, as he notices a small light which appears to be suspended in the air behind the mist. "C'mon," he says, as he walks in the light's direction.

The closer they get to the illuminated area, the more they can see that the light is coming from inside the top of a watch tower. The tower is connected to the adjacent stone, which is only a couple stories. It has winding steps and small rectangular windows.

"You – you think someone is in there?" Jesse stammers as he looks up at the tower.

Langston is pondering the same thing. "Don't know. But we don't have a choice but to find out. Who knows how far this bridge goes, and we need a break. Just stay quiet."

Cautiously they approach the steps and walk up the path, practically tiptoeing. A rickety door is at the top of the steps, and doesn't look like it will take much to open. Langston looks at Jesse, raising his eyebrows just before placing his hand on the door. He balls his other hand into a fist, ready to defend against whatever or whoever may be behind it.

Jesse's skin begins to sporadically change in color. He looks down at his hands with wide eyes.

"Breathe," Langston whispers.

Jesse nods. The door creaks as Langston pushes it, giving it just enough force for it to drift open. There isn't anyone inside. There is only a cot with a thin, used mattress; a lantern with a small flame. Empty bottles and trash are scattered in the room. Another smaller area is also nearby, which contains an empty, soiled bucket and debris.

On the walls are randomly hand-drawn pictures of various things, such as numbers, letters and flowers. It includes the Trillium flower that Langston had seen before. He rubs his fingers across the drawings, wondering what they all meant.

"Get some rest," Langston points to the cot after inspecting the space. "I will do the same."

Jesse finally exhales and walks briskly toward the cot. He doesn't think twice about Langston's instructions and hops on it. It practically dismantles from his weight, but stays up enough for him to enjoy it. He chuckles by the act, managing to form a small smile before turning on his side and drifting asleep.

Langston turns his attention to the lantern. He tries to blow out the flame, but the flame only reappears after each strong blow. Puzzled, he shrugs off the effort and decides to get some sleep, too. He doesn't need anything new to worry about. He takes some of the debris in the room – old clothing and papers - and balls them together. Forming a pillow, he lies on the floor.

Sometime later, Jesse is awoken by a noise. The sound doesn't appear to be close, from what he can tell; however, it it's gradually getting louder. He quietly gets up and runs to the smaller room. He relieves himself before approaching Langston who is now in a deep slumber.

"Mr. Langston. Mr. Langston." He shakes him a little. No response. He shakes him again. "I hear something."

Langston can barely get coherent before he quickly sits up and listens. Wiping the small bit of saliva from the side of his mouth, he props himself on one knee. He slowly peaks out the small tower windows to the bridge below. He sees someone but can't make out any details of the person.

"Stay quiet. Maybe they will pass us," Langston whispers to Jesse, without taking his eyes off the person approaching.

The two of them virtually hold their breaths as they watch the person approach. The person seems to be ready to walk past the tower, but then stops just beyond it to look at it. Langston ducks down and forces Jesse to do the same, while almost being seen. The person continues to walk but stops again and changes direction. They turn quickly toward the tower's entrance at the top of the steps.

Langston panics. He looks around to find anything he can use as a weapon. Grabbing the lantern first, he thinks he can somehow wield it; although, it is bolted down to the shaky, wooden table. He then notices that there is a loose piece of stone on one of the window panes. He struggles to loosen the stone more as the person's steps grow louder. He manages to free the stone just as the person arrives at the door.

He looks over at Jesse, who has managed to fully blend in with the wall behind them. Langston is shocked by Jesse's action, but maintains his focus.

There is an eerie pause between the time the door swings open and the time Langston reacts to it. The sound of subtle wind and water droplets moving is all that can be heard. Everything seems to be in slow motion, except for Langston's thoughts. He moves to the side of the door slowly, ready to defend against what appears to be a growing threat. Raising his hand some, he is readying the stone within his grip.

Suddenly, a familiar voice speaks. "My travels have strained me enough. Using that stone to harm me further is not necessary. I assure you."

Jesse slowly changes back into his normal appearance and moves away from the wall. Langston signals for him to stay back as he cautiously approaches the doorway.

"Come, come. Help an old man inside," the voice speaks again.

"The – the man from the house? Is that you?" Langston asks.

The man walks deeper into the room. He breathes heavily, taking a sip of water before he removes his hat. He dusts it off on the side of his leg. "Is that how you treat a new friend?"

"What are you doin' here?" Langston walks towards him briskly, extending his hand to assist the weary, old traveler. He guides him over to the cot Jesse had previously occupied, helping him sit without falling.

"Well, let's just say that my time in that house has expired."

"What does that mean? And what happened to your hand?"

The tired uncle - better known to Langston as the wise, gifted elder - has left his home and stumbled upon their whereabouts. They had been discovered by way of a brief exchange of information with locals in the Pines. He now shares space on the same bridge that Langston hopes leads to his home.

"Never mind my hand."

"But you said . . . to not *harm* you further? Who harmed you?"

"Never mind all of that!"

"Uh, okay," Langston replies.

"I apologize. I am tired and evidently a bit grumpy." The elder takes a moment to reset.

"It's okay."

"But I – I guess our relationship has graduated . . . to a new level of transparency," the elderly man replies. "I never thought that I would be here, and in this place with you. But here I am. Foremost, my name is Winston. It's only fair that you know my name, too. You are the first in many cycles to learn of my name."

"Why haven't you told anybody your name?" Jesse asks.

"Well, for one – I don't normally get many visitors. The few that I do get already know my name."

"Why did you follow us?" Langston interjects.

"I had visitors after you left my estate. More than I care to have. And not the type of company I wish to keep." The elder strokes his beard.

"Were they looking for me?" Langston asks.

"Some, yes. And they weren't too happy when I didn't have much information to give them."

Langston looks the old man over. "Did they hurt you?"

"No, no. Nothing that I can't handle. But the encounter motivated me to move on. I decided that it was time to get away from that city. Apparently I had not moved far away enough to begin with."

"I feel like you not tellin' me something,'" Langston responds.

The old man sighs as he positions himself in a more comfortable position. Removing the cloth on his hand, he pours water over his wound. He then reapplies the cloth and tightens it more. "I guess I will get right to it then. Please, just listen. I met some locals on my way here, and I heard some troubling news. It seems . . . it seems — I'm not quite sure how to say this."

"Just say it."

"If what I was told is the truth, it seems that humans – like you – have been some sort of subjects in an experiment."

"What kind of experiment?" Langston asks.

"I am not sure, but I have an idea. The original Guardian, whose counsel I served, loved his people. Even before the change, he loved his neighbors and his community. He held his city in high regard. Several cycles after the event and after Hock was built, he came up with a plan."

"A plans to do what?"

"His plan was to find a way to make everyone normal again; human again. Like you. He told me about his plan. I backed him with almost everything he wanted to do; but I knew that, with this idea, there would be push back. Some wouldn't agree. And I was right. His son, The Guardian who you met – Franklin- did everything in his power to rebel against his father's plan. I saw the rebellion growing in the early stages and decided that I would retire my services, and move away. I wanted no parts of a war on any level. My goal was to continue to advise him, but from a distance. I advised The Guardian to implement his plan in private, and he eventually agreed. But it was too late! Somehow, Franklin still found out." Winston becomes out of breath.

"But didn't The Guardian have the power to rule over Franklin? How – why did he just let him take over?"

"A father's love for his child can be blinding. He couldn't bring himself to do anything to his son. He would rather agree and comply than harm his child."

"So what Franklin told me is a lie . . ."

"What did Franklin tell you?"

"He said that The Guardian–"

Winston huffs before interrupting, "You know what? I don't want to know what Franklin said, because Franklin is a liar. He has been a liar ever since he was a kid. Don't trust anything he says. If we continue to repeat untruths, the truth will be buried."

"Honestly, I hope I never see him again."

"Me too," Jesse chimes in. He sits, folding his legs underneath him.

"I believe Franklin is behind these experiments. The Guardian wanted a normal society. He wanted things the way they were, as much as possible. But Franklin didn't agree. He challenged him on everything."

"What does Franklin have to gain by going against him about this?"

"That is a good question. Did you look around while you were in that city? Greed! He lusts his power and wants to keep it, amongst other reasons. All I know is . . . the experiments are not working. The humans being tested are dying. They are throwing them out into the wilderness when the tests fail, like meat to wolves. Do you understand?"

"Yes." Langston folds his arms. He envisions what the testing process might look like. *Horrible,* he thinks.

"Which brings me to you . . ."

"What about me?"

"Think, young Langston. Think. You were found out there by Jesse, yes?" The old man leans forward with growing excitement.

"Um, yeah."

"What else do you remember? Can you remember anything before the moment?"

"Not really. I just know I was in a hospital gown when he found me."

"Yeah! And Mr. Langston almost fell off the bridge. Right out there when we got here. He was screaming." Jesse stands up and leans on the loose window pane ledge. He tries to look out at the bridge but the window is fogged. Using his finger, he makes a small circle to see through.

"What is he talking about, Langston?"

"Kind of embarrassing to say. " Langston lowers his head and strokes his forehead with his fingers.

"Ha! After all you have experienced, why do you care?"

Langston shrugs, "Right before we found this tower, something happened. I still don't know what it was. I felt sharp pains, like someone was stabbing or poking me. I – I blacked out, I guess. It felt like someone had me and was holding me down."

"Oh my," the elderly man sits back and holds his face. "A hospital gown? Sharp pains? Don't you see? You – you are one of the humans they were testing!"

Langston begins to pace. "No. I would remem . . . - you think?"

"How else would you explain your scattered memory? The gown? Waking up in the middle of nowhere? And how do you know it was a hospital gown? Have you ever been to a hospital?"

Langston doesn't know how to respond. Winston's questions were coming at him too rapidly for him to handle. He continues to rub his head, as if he is trying to rub out a memory or two. His eyes feel watery.

Jesse listens, trying to understand everything being said. His mind dances between where the three of them rest now versus what he would be doing on a normal day. A quick run or two, bringing old jewelry, clothing and recyclables back to Hock.

"But there is more," Langston speaks with certainty.

"More?"

"When we were in The Guardian's cellar, I had a dream."

"Go on," Winston replies.

"It wasn't a long dream, but -"

"What happened in the dream?"

"I was a kid. My mother and a man was talking. I guess . . . I guess he was my father. They were arguing."

"Is that all you can remember?"

Langston paces more, mouthing some things to himself, while clearly thinking aloud.

Before Langston can respond, Winston pats him on the leg. "Don't worry, my friend. Together, we can figure out what's going on. Together, we can get you home and begin to piece these things together." He then turns his attention toward Jesse. "As for you – you deserve a better childhood. There is a greater plan for you, too. I'm sure of it."

"What about Kinth? Miles?" Langston sighs. He approaches the tower windows and looks out.

"Madam Pearl," Jesse adds softly.

"I feel like everyone is in trouble because of me," Langston adds.

Winston stands as quickly as his tired, bewildered frame will allow. "Langston, do not blame yourself. Do not go down that path. Once you begin a guilt trip, you never return. That trip will leave you sad and alone. Learn to make peace with your decisions. Besides, you did not start this. But we – we will finish it."

"So this means you are coming with us?" Jesse asks.

"I have come to realize that your journey is the journey of many. Helping you not only *helps* you, but helps me and many others. So yes. Rest up, because we will continue this path soon."

Langston exhales as a tear slowly rolls down his cheek.

"When we awake, I have more information to share with you. I am tired and need to rest."

"Thank you," Langston says softly, with a turn of relief. He watches Winston drift asleep.

He wonders what is next, as he looks beyond the tower and the bridge. He has come so far, but he feels like his journey is far from over.

C. SCHMIDT

If you enjoyed Uhmandra,

here are other works by C. Schmidt:

"Hock City"

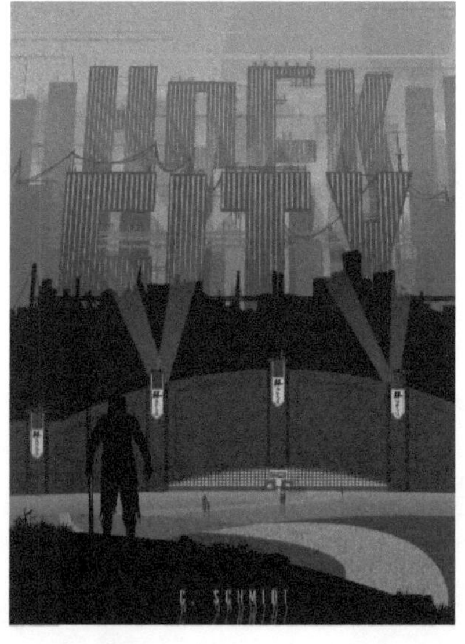

Available at various book retailers!